# THE
# BUMPER HIGHLY
# DANGEROUS
# JOKE BOOK

*The Green and Hairy Joke Book* first published 1987 by Magnet
The *Yellow and Highly Dangerous Joke Book* first published 1989 by Magnet
*The Pink and Wobbly Joke Book* first published 1990 by Mammoth
*The Purple and Spotty Joke Book* first published 1991 by Mammoth

This edition published 1993 by Dean,
an imprint of Reed Consumer Books Limited
Michelin House, 81 Fulham Road, London SW3 6RB
and Auckland, Melbourne, Singapore and Toronto

Text copyright © Martyn Forrester 1987, 1989, 1990,1991
Illustrations copyright © Tony Blundell 1987, 1989, 1990, 1991

ISBN 0 603 55134 3

Printed in Great Britain by The Bath Press

# THE BUMPER HIGHLY DANGEROUS JOKE BOOK

## Al Caprawn

## *with cartoons by Tony Blundell*

DEAN

# THE GREEN AND HAIRY JOKE BOOK

Knock, knock,
– *Who's there?*
Lettuce.
– *Lettuce who?*
Lettuce tell you
a few good green
and hairy jokes.

**Customer:** Have you any wild gooseberries?
**Waiter:** No sir, but we can take some ordinary ones and irritate them for you.

Should you eat gooseberries with your fingers?

*No, fingers should be eaten separately.*

**Customer:** Why is my piece of gooseberry pie all smashed?
**Waiter:** Well, you said 'Fetch a piece of gooseberry pie, and step on it.'

**Bert:** My dad went to pick some gooseberries last night, slipped, and broke his leg.
**Fred:** That's terrible. What did your mother do?
**Bert:** She opened a tin of peaches instead.

When do elephants paint their toe-nails green?

*When they want to hide upside-down in a pot of gooseberry jam.*

**Man in restaurant:** Will you join me in a piece of gooseberry pie?
**Woman:** Do you think there's room for both of us?

**Man on train:** Excuse me, I think you're sitting in my seat.
**Woman:** Can you prove it?
**Man:** I think so. You see, I left a big piece of gooseberry pie on it.

Why are gooseberry seeds like gateposts?

*Because they propagate.*

Why is a Boy Scout like a tin of gooseberries?

*They are both prepared.*

What's green and smells?

*Kermit's nose.*

What's green and hairy and flies a UFO?

*A Martian gooseberry.*

What's green and hairy and takes aspirins?

*A gooseberry with a headache.*

What's green and hairy and coughs?

*A gooseberry with a bad chest.*

What's green and hairy and sits on the sea bed?

*A gooseberry in a submarine.*

What do you get if you cross
a gooseberry with a tiger?

*I don't know — but I wouldn't
try eating it!*

What do you call a gooseberry
who insults a farmer?

*Fresh fruit.*

What do you get if you cross a
gooseberry with an elephant?

*A pie that never forgets.*

What do you get if you cross a gooseberry with an aeroplane?

*Pie in the sky.*

What do you get if you cross a gooseberry with an alligator?

*A gooseberry that bites back.*

What do you get if you cross two gooseberries with a banana skin?

*A pair of green slippers.*

What do you get if you cross
a bowl of gooseberries with
a pair of roller skates?

*Meals on wheels.*

What do you get if you cross
a gooseberry with an elk?

*Gooseberry mousse.*

What do you get if you cross
a gooseberry with an idiot?

*Gooseberry fool.*

Two ants were in a supermarket.
They climbed up on a shelf and on
to a box containing a gooseberry
pie. Suddenly the first ant began
running.

'Wait for me!' cried the other ant.
'What's the hurry?'

'Can't you read?' said the first.
'It says here: TEAR ALONG THE
DOTTED LINE.'

What is green and hairy and
extremely dangerous?

*A herd of stampeding gooseberries.*

How do you stop a herd of
stampeding gooseberries from
charging?

*Take away their credit cards.*

What do you get if you cross
the M1 with a gooseberry?

*Run over.*

What is green and bald outside,
and green and hairy inside?

*An inside-out gooseberry.*

What is red outside, green and
hairy inside, and very crowded?

*A bus full of gooseberries.*

**Girl:** Try some of this gooseberry tart
I've just made.
**Boy:** Ugh, it's awful!
**Girl:** You're wrong. It definitely says
in my cookery book that this recipe
is delicious.

**Man in café:**
I don't like this
gooseberry
pie.
**Woman
cook:** Well,
I'll have you
know I was
making
gooseberry
pies before
you were
born.
**Man:**
Perhaps this
is one of
them.

A tramp knocked on a door and asked
the lady of the house for some food.
'Didn't I give you a slice of my home-
made gooseberry tart a week ago?'
she asked.
'Yes,' said the tramp, 'but I'm a lot
better now.'

What's green
and hairy
and red
all over?

*An embarrassed
gooseberry.*

**Teacher:** How do you spell
'gooseberry'?
**Pupil:** G-u-z-b-r-y.
**Teacher:** The dictionary spells it
g-o-o-s-e-b-e-r-r-y.
**Pupil:** You didn't ask me how the
dictionary spells it!

**Teacher:** If I had forty gooseberries
in one hand,
and forty in
the other,
what would
I have?
**Pupil:** Big hands.

What did the dentist say when his wife baked a gooseberry pie?

*'Can I do the filling?'*

What's the difference between a gooseberry and an elephant?

*A gooseberry is green.*

*       *       *

What did Hannibal say when he saw the elephants coming?

**'Here come the gooseberries' – he was colour-blind!**

What's the difference between a gooseberry, a gorilla, and a tube of glue?
– *I don't know.*
Well, you can bite into a gooseberry, but you can't bite into a gorilla.
– *What about the tube of glue?*
I thought that was where you'd get stuck!

Why is a gooseberry green and hairy?

*Because if it was white and bald, it would be a Mint Imperial.*

What's blue and hairy?

*A gooseberry holding its breath.*

What did one gooseberry bush say to the other gooseberry bush?

*Take me to your weeder.*

What did one gooseberry say to the other gooseberry?

*Nothing. Gooseberries can't talk.*

What's the best thing to put into a gooseberry pie?

*Your teeth.*

What's green and hairy and
wears sunglasses?

*A gooseberry on holiday.*

What is a gooseberry's skin
most used for?

*To keep the gooseberry together.*

How do you stop a gooseberry
ripening on a Saturday?

*Pick it on Friday.*

What do you get if you cross
a river with a giant gooseberry?

*To the other side.*

What do you get if you cross
a river with an ordinary gooseberry?

*Wet.*

Why did the man have to go to hospital
after the gooseberry fell on his
head?

*It was in a tin.*

What side of a gooseberry is the hairiest?

*The outside.*

What does a gooseberry do when it's raining?

*Gets wet.*

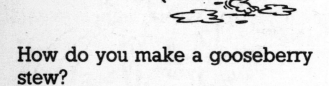

How do you make a gooseberry stew?

*Keep it waiting for two hours.*

What did the green gooseberry say to the blue gooseberry?

*'Cheer up!'*

What's the difference between a gooseberry and a worm?

*Ever tried eating worm pie?*

What's the difference between a gooseberry and an elephant?

*Pick them up – an elephant is usually heavier.*

What's green and hairy and
goes up and down?

*A gooseberry in a lift.*

What did the gooseberry say
to the hungry maggot?

*You're boring me.*

What did the gooseberry say
to the greenfly?

*You really bug me.*

What do you call a two-ton
gooseberry with a nasty temper?

'Sir!'

What do you have when 2,000
gooseberries try to get through a door
together?

Gooseberry jam.

What do you get when you cross
a gooseberry with a chicken?

A hen that lays green and hairy
eggs.

Where do you find wild gooseberries?

*It depends where they were lost.*

If your cat ate an unripe gooseberry, what would she become?

*A sourpuss.*

What is green and hairy, has one bionic eye, and fights crime?

*The Six-Million-Dollar Gooseberry.*

Where do giant gooseberries come from?

*Giant gooseberry bushes.*

What is the best way to keep gooseberries?

*Don't return them.*

What's green and hairy and goes round and round?

*A gooseberry in a spin.*

What's enormous and yellow,
and says 'Fe-fi-fo-fum?'

*A giant lemon.*

What's yellow and goes slam,
slam, slam, slam?

*A four-door lemon.*

What's yellow, has four doors, and
goes beep, beep, beeeeeeeeep?

*A lemon with a jammed horn.*

How do you make a lemon drop?

*Shake the tree hard.*

What's
yellow
and goes
thump,
squish,
thump,
squish?

*A lemon
with
one
wet
plimsoll.*

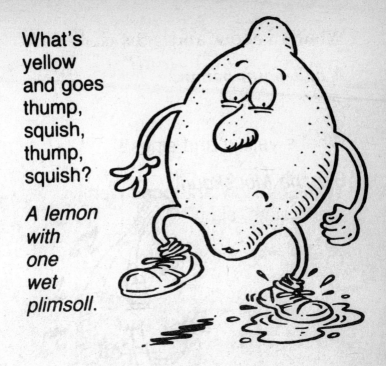

Why did Cinderella's fairy
godmother change the pumpkin
into a coach?

*She didn't have a lemon handy.*

What's yellow and goes click-click?

*A ball-point banana.*

What's yellow and sings?

*Banana Mouskouri.*

What's yellow on the inside and green on the outside?

*A banana disguised as a cucumber.*

What's yellow, wears a cape, and fights crime?

*Superbanana.*

What's yellow and hums?

*An electric banana.*

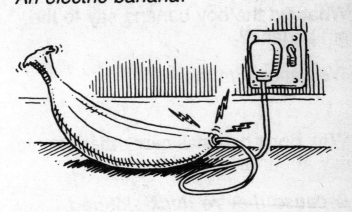

What's yellow and goes putt-putt?

*An outboard banana.*

Why is a banana skin like a pullover?

*They're both easy to slip on.*


Why did the banana split?

*Because it saw the apple turnover.*


Why didn't the banana snore?

*Because it was afraid of waking up the rest of the bunch.*


What did the boy banana say to the girl banana?

*'You appeal to me.'*


Why don't bananas care what people say about them?

*Because they're thick-skinned.*

Where should a twenty-pound banana go?

*On a diet.*

What is the easiest way to make a banana split?

*Cut it in half.*

When an apple hits a banana, what is it called?

*A fruit punch.*

**What's big and yellow and lives in Scotland?**

*The Loch Ness Banana.*

What do
you do
with a
green
banana?

*Teach it
something.*

**Teacher?** If I cut two bananas and
two apples into ten pieces each, what
will I get?
**Pupil:** A fruit salad.

**Why don't bananas have dandruff?**

*Did you ever see a banana with
hair?*

What's yellow, washable, dries
quickly and doesn't need ironing?

*A drip-dry banana.*

What's green, covered in custard, and moans a lot?

*Gooseberry grumble.*

How can you tell when there's an elephant in your custard?

*By the lumps.*

What's yellow and can't count to 10?

*Thick custard.*

Did you hear about the man who stole some gooseberries?

*He was put into custardy.*

'Waiter, is there custard on the menu?'

*'No sir, I wiped it off.'*

A man saw a gardener pushing a wheel-barrow full of manure.
'Where are you going with that?' he asked.
'I'm going to put it on my gooseberries,' said the gardener.
'Suit yourself,' the man replied.
'I usually put custard on mine.'

What's yellow and highly dangerous?

*Shark-infested custard.*

What flies around the kitchen at 600mph and glows yellow?

*An Unidentified Flying Omelette.*

'Tough luck,' said the egg in the monastery.
'Out of the frying-pan, into the friar!'

Knock knock.
– *Who's there?*
Egbert.
– *Egbert who?*
Egbert no bacon.


What's yellow and white and travels at 90mph?
*A train-driver's egg sandwich.*

Why did the egg go into the jungle?
*It was an eggsplorer.*


If an egg came floating down the Mississippi River where would it have come from?
*A chicken.*

**What's white
and fluffy
and swings
from cake-shop
to cake-shop?**

*A meringue-utang.*

What's white and fluffy, has
whiskers, and floats?

*A cata-meringue.*

What is purple and crazy?

*A grape nut.*

What is a raisin?

*A grape with a lot of worries.*

What's round and purple
and bad at cooking?

*Alfred the Grape.*

What's big, purple and
lies in the sea?

*Grape Britain.*

What's purple and lives
in South America?

*A Grape Train Robber.*

What's purple and burns?

*The Grape Fire of London.*

What's purple and swings through the trees?

*Tarzan of the Grapes.*

What's purple and 4,000 miles long?

*The Grape Wall of China.*

What was purple and ruled the world?

*Alexander the Grape.*

What's purple and round and floats up
in the sky?

*The Planet of the Grapes.*

**What American lakes are filled with
purple juice?**

*The Grape Lakes.*

What did the grape
say when the
elephant trod on it?

*Nothing – it just gave
a little wine.*

What sits in a fruit bowl
and shouts for help?

*A damson in distress.*

**Who was purple and discovered
America in 1492?**

*Christopher Plumbus.*

Which was the smallest plum?

*Tom Plum.*

Why does a plum make a good
museum-keeper?

*Plum preserves.*

What should you do if your
pet plum falls ill?

*Call the plumber.*

Who is purple, rides a motorbike,
and jumps over buses?

*Evel Plumevel.*

Why did the plum go into hospital?

*He was plum crazy.*

**Why did the apple turnover?**

*Because it saw the Swiss roll.*

**Why wouldn't the man eat apples?**

*Because his granny had died of apple-plexy.*

**What animals in Noah's Ark didn't come in pairs?**

*Worms, they came in apples.*

**What do you call a Welsh apple?**

*Taffy apple.*

'Mum, can I have some money for the old man crying outside in the street?'
'Of course, son. What's he crying about?'
'Toffee apples – for sale!'


Confucius, he say: An apple a day keeps the doctor away – if aimed correctly.

When is an apple not an apple?

*When it is a crab.*

Did Adam and Eve ever have a date?

*No, they had an apple.*

'What are you doing in my apple tree, young man?
'One of your apples fell down, sir, and I'm putting it back.'

What lives in apples and is an avid reader?

*A bookworm.*

What do you get when you cross an apple with a Christmas tree?

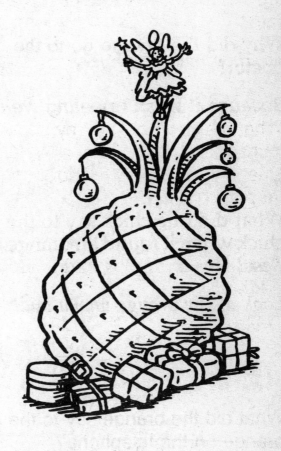

*A pine-apple.*

What do you get if you cross a citrus fruit with a bell?

*An orange that can peal itself.*

Why did the orange go to the doctor?

*Because it wasn't peeling well.*

What did one chick say to the other chick when it found an orange in the nest?

*Look at the orange mama laid!*

What did the orange say to the other orange on the telephone?

*Nothing, the pips went.*

Why couldn't the orange get up the hill?

*Because it had run out of juice.*

What does a vegetarian vampire eat?

*Blood oranges.*

**What do you get when you cross an orange and a squash court?**

*Orange squash.*

**What do you do with a hurt lemon?**

*Give it lemon-aid.*

What is a tangerine?

*An orange in an easy-open wrapper.*

What was the orange doing
in a palm tree?

*It had heard that coconuts
have more fun.*

**Why are oranges and lemons
safe from pickpockets?**

*They don't have pockets.*

What did one strawberry say to the other strawberry?

*Between you and me, we shouldn't be in this jam.*

What do farmers do to endangered strawberries?

*Put them in preserves.*

Did you hear the story about the world's biggest strawberry?

*No.*

Never mind, it's over your head.

How can you tell that strawberries are lazy?

*They spend their entire lives in beds.*

What is rhubarb?

*Celery with high blood pressure.*

What is red and wears a mask?

*The Lone Raspberry.*

What do you call an overweight pumpkin?

*A plumpkin.*

Why is history the sweetest lesson?

*Because it's full of dates.*

**What's a good way of putting on weight?**

*Eat a peach, swallow the centre, and you've gained a stone.*

What do you call a peach that is green and skinny at harvest time?

*A failure.*

What did the girl say after she ate a basket of fresh peaches?

*'Burp!'*

How were Humpty Dumpty and the peach with a weak stem alike?

*They both had a great fall.*

\*     \*     \*

Why wouldn't the ripe peach sit on the wall?

*It had heard what happened to Humpty Dumpty.*

How do you tell a peach from a Jumbo jet?

*A peach's tank is too small for it to cross the Atlantic without refuelling.*

**What is a prickly pear?**

*Two porcupines.*

Knock, knock.
– *Who's there?*
Pear.
– *Pear who?*
Pair of shoes.


Knock, knock.
– *Who's there?*
Shoes.
– *Shoes who?*
Shoes me, I didn't mean to tread on your pear.

What do you call twins whose mother is a peach and whose father is a pear?

*A peach of a pair.*

What is the difference between a pear and an elephant?

*A pear always forgets.*

*       *       *

Why do pears always forget?

*What do they have to remember?*

What's the biggest nut
in the British Army?

*The kernel.*

What nut sounds like
a sneeze?

*Cashew!*

Why did the peanut complain
to the police?

*Because he was a salted.*

How do you know peanuts are
fattening?

*Have you ever seen a skinny
elephant?*

What nut has no shell?

*A doughnut.*

What do you call it when monkeys throw coconuts at each other?

*Gorilla warfare!*

**Which nut invaded Britain?**

*William the Conker.*

What's brown and chocolatey outside, has a peanut inside, and sings hymns?

*A Sunday School Treet.*

What's brown, woolly, covered in chocolate, and goes round the sun?

*A Mars Baaaaaa!*

**Mother:** There were two Mars bars in the larder yesterday, and now there's only one. Why?
**Son:** It must have been so dark I didn't see the other one.

**What did the chocolate bar say to the lollipop?**

*Hi-ya, sucker!*

**What's brown and hairy, and bashful?**

*A coconut shy.*

**What's brown and hairy, and coughs?**

*A coconut with a bad chest.*

**What's brown, and eaten by French people for breakfast?**

*Huit heures bix.*

How many cabbages can you put in an empty sack?

*One. After that, the sack isn't empty.*

Why didn't the boy eat his spinach after his mother told him it would put colour in his cheeks?

*He didn't want green cheeks.*

What sort of vegetables do plumbers fix?

*Leeks.*

What's the difference between mouldy lettuce and a dismal song?

*One is a bad salad, and the other a sad ballad.*

What do you call a vegetable's wages?

*His celery.*

**Teacher** (on school dinner duty): Any complaints?

**Pupil:** Yes sir, these peas are too hard.

**Teacher** (taking a spoonful and tasting them): They seem soft enough to me.

**Pupil:** They are now. I've been chewing them for the last half hour.

What grows in the garden and is a Kung Fu expert?

*Bruce Leek.*

What's green and very fast?

*A runner bean.*

What's green, weighs a ton, and can float in a glass of Martini?

*An olivephant.*

What's green and plays snooker?

*A cue-cumber.*

What's big and green, has four legs, and if it fell out of a tree would kill you?

*A snooker table.*

What's the difference between a market gardener and a billiard-player?

*One minds his peas, and the other minds his cues.*

Why did the carrot colour itself green?

*So it could hide in the cucumber patch.*

*       *       *

Did you ever see a carrot in a cucumber patch?

*See – the disguise worked.*

What is the poorest plant?

*A vine, because it cannot support itself.*

What does a vegetarian cannibal eat?

*Swedes.*

What vegetable should you pick to go with jacket potatoes?

*Button mushrooms.*

**What do you get if you cross rabbits with leeks?**

*Bunions.*

Two ears of corn were running up a hill. What were they when they got to the top?

*Puffed wheat.*

How do you make jumping beans?

*Go up behind them and shout 'Boo'!*

What do you call two turnips who fall in love?

*Swedehearts.*

What is green, curly, and shy?

*Lettuce alone.*

What is green, curly, and goes around at 100mph?

*A Lettuce Elan.*

What is green, curly, and religious?

*Lettuce pray.*

Why was the farmer cross?

*Because someone trod on his corn.*

Is it true that carrots are good for the eyesight?

*Well, you never see rabbits wearing glasses.*

How do you find a lost rabbit?

*Make a noise like a big carrot.*

What's long, orange and shoots rabbits?

*A double-barrelled carrot.*

Doctor, doctor, I've got carrots
growing out of my ears!
*How on earth did that happen?*
I don't know – I planted cucumbers.

**Bert:** Why do you have carrots
sticking out of your ears?
**Fred:** You'll have to talk louder. I have
carrots sticking out of my ears.

Why did the farmer run a
steamroller over his potato patch?

*Because he wanted mashed potatoes.*

Did you hear about the farmer who
planted his potatoes with razor blades
in them? He wanted to grow chips.

How do you make a potato puff?

*Chase it around the garden.*

What do hedgehogs have for dinner?

*Prickled onions.*

What garden plant has eyes but never needs glasses?

*The potato.*

What do you get if you cross a potato with an onion?

*A spud with watery eyes.*

What happened to the potato that refused to work?

*It was sacked.*

Where do you find chilli beans?

*At the North Pole.*

How did the green cabbage talk to the lettuce?

*Head to head.*


Why did the police arrest the green cabbage?

*It was involved in a garden plot.*

Why was the green cabbage disliked by all the other vegetables?

*It had a big head.*

How can you tell an apple from a green cabbage?

*If it's red it's probably an apple.*

Knock, knock.
– *Who's there?*
Beets.
– *Beets who?*
Beets me, I just forgot the joke.

Knock, knock.
– *Who's there.*
Bean.
– *Bean who?*
Bean working hard lately.

**Why did the grey elephant sit on the red tomato?**

*It wanted to play squash.*

**What's round, red and cheeky?**

*Tomato sauce.*

**What can a whole red tomato do but half a red tomato can't?**

*Look round.*

Why did the tomato go red?

*Because it saw the salad dressing.*

Why was the red tomato in such a hurry?

*It wanted to ketchup.*

What is a vampire's favourite soup?

*Scream of tomato.*

What's green and holds up stage coaches?

*Dick Gherkin.*

What's short and green and goes camping?

*A Boy Sprout.*

What's green and goes boing-boing?

*Spring cabbage.*

What's green, seven feet tall, and mopes in the corner?

*The Incredible Sulk.*

\*       \*       \*

What's green and wrinkled?

*The Incredible Sulk's granny.*

How do you make golden
vegetable soup?

*Use fourteen carats.*


There were two tomatoes on
horseback. Which was the cowboy?

*Neither – they were both redskins.*


Why shouldn't
you tell
secrets in
a vegetable
garden?

*Because corn
has ears,
and beans talk.*

What's orange
and comes out
of the ground
at 100mph?

*A jet-propelled
carrot.*

'Doctor, can you give me something
for my liver?'

*'How about a pound of onions?'*

How do you calculate the colour of a cabbage?

*Use a green gauge.*

What stands on one leg and has its heart in its head?

*A cabbage.*

What's the quickest way across the vegetable patch?

*The dual cabbage-way.*

What did the cabbage say when he knocked on the door?

*'Lettuce in.'*

Why are large cabbages generous?

*Because they have big hearts.*

What's green and round and points North?

*A magnetic cabbage.*

**Baby Cabbage:** Mummy, where did I come from?

**Mummy Cabbage:** The stalk brought you, dear.

What magazine do vegetable growers read?

*The Weeder's Digest.*

What's green and slimy and
is found at the North Pole?

*A lost frog.*

What's green and slimy and
highly dangerous?

*A frog with a machine-gun.*

What do frogs drink?

*Croaka-Cola.*

What's green with red spots?

*A frog with measles.*

What happens to a frog's car when it breaks down?

*It gets toad away.*

Where do frogs leave their coats at the theatre?

*In the croakroom.*

What ballet is most popular with frogs?

*Swamp Lake.*

What's white outside, green inside,
and hops?

*A frog sandwich.*

Where do frogs go when they've got
bad eyesight?

*To a hoptician.*

What do you call a girl with a frog on
her head?

*Lily.*

**What do you call a frog spy?**

*A croak and dagger agent.*

What's green and slimy and
lives in a lighthouse?

*A frog-horn.*

What's green and slimy and red?

*A frog with sunburn.*

What is bright blue, weighs a ton, has four legs and talks?

*Two half-ton parrots.*

What colours would you paint
the sun and the wind?

*The sun rose and the wind blew.*

'That's a strange pair of socks you've
got on – one dark blue and one light
blue.'

*'I know – I've got another pair just
like it at home.'*

What's blue and yellow and has a
wingspan of 60 feet?

*A three-ton budgie.*

Have you any blue ties to match my
eyes?

*No, but we've got some soft hats to
match your head.*

What goes in green and comes out blue?

*A gooseberry swimming on a cold day.*

Why did the policeman wear indigo braces?

*To keep his trousers up.*

**Sherlock Holmes:** Ah, Watson, you are wearing your violet thermal underpants today . . .

**Dr Watson:** Absolutely astounding, Holmes! How on earth did you deduce that?

**Sherlock Holmes:** Elementary, my dear Watson. You forgot to put on your trousers.


What's blue and round and has eight wheels?

*A blueberry on roller-skates.*

I heard a good green and hairy joke and was going to take it home, but I decided that that was carrying a joke too far.

What's got twenty-two legs and goes "Slurp, slurp, slurp"?
*A football team eating strawberry blancmange.*

What's pink and wobbly and indestructible?
*The Six Million Dollar Strawberry Blancmange.*

What's bright blue and wobbly?
*A bowl of strawberry blancmange holding its breath.*

What's pink and wobbly and heavy?
*Strawberry blancmange made with
cement.*

What's grey, weighs four tons, and
leaves footprints in the strawberry
blancmange?
*An elephant in the fridge.*

What did the strawberry blancmange
say to the elephant?
*Nothing – strawberry blancmange can't
talk.*

What's pink and wobbly and comes from Mars?
*A Martian mallow.*

What's pink and wobbly and fights crime?
*Super Blancmange.*

What's green and wobbly?
*A bowl of seasick blancmange.*

What do you do with a bowl of blue strawberry blancmange?
*Try to cheer it up.*

What's pink and goes "Wobble, wobble, bang"?
*A bowl of strawberry blancmange in a minefield.*

What's pink and wobbly and goes up and down twenty times a day?
*A bowl of strawberry blancmange doing press-ups.*

What's pink and wobbly and hangs out your underpants?
*Your mum.*

What's pink and wobbly and belongs to grandad?
*Grandma.*

What's pink and wobbly and goes
"ABC . . . slurp . . . DEF . . .
slurp"?
*Grandma eating alphabet soup.*

What's pink and wobbly and grows
under your nose?
*Tulips.*

What's small, pink and eats cakes?
*A pink dwarf cake-eater.*

What's pink and white, comes out
at night, and sings in a high voice?
*Falsetto teeth.*

What's green and wobbly and plays
rock music?
*Electric catarrh.*

What's green and wobbly and hangs
from trees?
*Giraffe snot.*

What's pink and wobbly and jumps
up and down?
*A bowl of strawberry blancmange at a
discotheque.*

What is as big as a bowl of strawberry blancmange and weighs nothing?
*A bowl of strawberry blancmange's shadow.*

What's pink and wobbly and travels at 110mph?
*A turbo-charged bowl of strawberry blancmange.*

What's pink and wobbly and green?
*A bowl of strawberry blancmange with a runny nose.*

What's pink and wobbly and green and brown?
*A bowl of strawberry blancmange with a runny nose in a muddy field.*

What's pink and wobbly, sits in the fridge and is highly dangerous?
*A bowl of strawberry blancmange with a machine gun.*

What's pink and wobbly and sits in the corner?
*A naughty bowl of strawberry blancmange.*

What's pink and wobbly, with red spots?
*A bowl of strawberry blancmange with measles.*

What's pink and wobbly and has a trunk?
*A bowl of strawberry blancmange going on holiday.*

What's pink and wobbly and swims
under the sea?
*A bowl of strawberry blancmange with an
aqualung.*

What's pink and wobbly and
noisy?
*A bowl of strawberry blancmange
with a set of drums.*

What's red and runs at 100mph?
*A bionic nose.*

What's red, round and cheeky?
*Tomato sauce.*

What's red and gives you the pips?
*A telephone box.*

What's red, hunted and blows up
buildings?
*Guy Fox.*

What's red, spreads and shouldn't
be broken?
*A rash promise.*

What's red and squashy and says
"Pardon"?
*A polite strawberry with hiccups.*

What's pink and wobbly and can't
stand still?
*A pig in a tumble drier.*

What's red and white and full of
policemen?
*A sunburnt Panda.*

What would you get if all the cars in
Britain were red?
*A red carnation.*

Why is getting up at five o'clock in
the morning like a pig's tail?
*Because it's twirly.*

What do you give a sick pig?
*Oinkment.*

**What do you call pigs who live
together?**
*Pen friends.*

PUPIL: Can you spell blind pig?
TEACHER: B-l-i-n-d p-i-g.
PUPIL: Wrong, it's b-l-n-d p-g. With two i's he wouldn't be blind.

DINER: Waiter, this meat isn't fit for a pig.
WAITER: I'll take it back, sir, and bring you some that is.

What does a pig use to write his letters with?
*Pen and oink.*

Who led 10,000 pigs up a hill and back down again?
*The Grand Old Duke of Pork.*

What do you call a pig thief?
*A hamburglar.*

Where do rich pigs live in America?
*In a sty scraper.*

Why is a leg of pork like an old radio?
*Because both of them have a lot of crackling.*

What happened to the piglet who studied Shakespeare?
*He ended up in Hamlet.*

What do you call a pig running around with no clothes on?
*Streaky bacon.*

What do you get if you cross a pig with a drummer?
*Ham rolls.*

What would happen if pigs could fly?
*Bacon would go up.*

Why should you never tell a secret to a pig?
*Because they're all squealers.*

What's pink and wobbly and plays football?
*Queen's Pork Rangers.*

What do you call it when pigs do their laundry?
*Hogwash.*

What do you get if you cross a pig with a young goat?
*A dirty kid.*

How do you take a sick pig to hospital?
*In a hambulance.*

Why didn't the piglets listen to their grandfather?
*Because he was an old boar.*

Why does a baby pig eat so much?
*To make a hog of itself.*

What did one pig say to the other pig?
*"Let's be pen pals."*

What do you get if you cross a pig with a flea?
*Pork scratchings.*

What is a pig's favourite ballet?
*Swine Lake.*

Why is the pig one of the unluckiest
animals in the farmyard?
*Because it is killed before it is cured.*

What do you get if you cross the M1
with a pig?
*A roadhog.*

How is a pig like a horse?
*When a pig is hungry it eats like a
horse, and when a horse is hungry
it eats like a pig.*

How did Mighty Pig explain his
success as an actor?
*"I ham what I ham."*

What's green and wobbly?
*A seasick pig.*

What is pigskin for?
*Holding a pig together.*

What kind of ties do pigs wear?
*Pig sties.*

Why did Cinderella's fairy
godmother turn a pumpkin into a
coach?
*She didn't have a strawberry
handy.*

Why did the policeman arrest the
strawberry?
*It was involved in a garden plot.*

How do you work out the colour of a strawberry?
*With a green gauge.*

Why did the strawberry plant cry?
*Because everyone was picking on it.*

TEACHER: If I cut two strawberries and two apples into ten pieces each, what will I get?
PUPIL: A fruit salad.

Why did the baby strawberry cry?
*Because his mother was in a jam.*

What do farmers do to endangered
strawberries?
*Put them in preserves.*

Did you hear the story about the
world's biggest strawberry?
*Never mind, it's over your head.*

How can you tell that strawberries are lazy?
*They spend their entire lives in beds.*

What's red and juicy with special powers?
*The Six Million Dollar Strawberry.*

What's red and juicy, costs a fortune, and has her own TV programme?
*The Bionic Strawberry.*

What's red and juicy and goes round and round?
*A strawberry in a spin-drier.*

What's red and juicy and wears
sunglasses?
*A strawberry on holiday.*

What did the strawberry say to the
hungry maggot?
*"You're boring me."*

What did the strawberry say to the
greenfly?
*"You really bug me."*

What do you have when two
thousand strawberries try to get
through a door together?
*Strawberry jam.*

If a strawberry hits a peach in the mouth, what is it?
*A fruit punch.*

Why is a strawberry a good museum keeper?
*Strawberry preserves.*

Why didn't the strawberry snore?
*Because it was afraid of waking up everyone else in the bed.*

Why did the raspberry jelly wobble?
*Because it saw the strawberry milkshake.*

What's red and points north?
*A magnetic strawberry.*

What's red and points south?
*A stupid magnetic strawberry.*

Why did the strawberry go out with
the prune?
*Because he couldn't find a date.*

What's red and goes up and down?
*A strawberry in a lift.*

What's enormous and red and says
"Fe-fi-fo-fum"?
*A giant strawberry.*

What's red, wears a cape, and fights crime?
*Superstrawberry.*

What's red and goes click-click?
*A ball-point strawberry.*

What's pink and wobbly and wears dark glasses?
*A bowl of strawberry blancmange in disguise.*

What happened to the man who couldn't tell putty from strawberry blancmange?
*His windows fell out.*

What's red outside, pink inside, and very crowded?
*A bus full of strawberry blancmange.*

What's pink and wobbly and comes at you from all sides?
*Stereophonic strawberry blancmange.*

What's pink and highly dangerous?
*Shark-infested strawberry blancmange.*

Why did the man have to go to hospital
after the strawberry blancmange fell on
his head?
*It was in a tin.*

What's pink and stupid?
*Thick strawberry blancmange.*

Why do elephants paint their toe-
nails pink?
*So they can hide upside down in
strawberry blancmange.*

What's pink and highly
dangerous?
*Kamikaze strawberry blancmange.*

If you have a referee in boxing, a
referee in football, and a referee in
rugby, what do you have in bowls?
*Strawberry blancmange.*

How can you tell when there's an elephant in your strawberry blancmange?
*When it's especially lumpy.*

What's pink and wobbly and has four wheels?
*A bowl of strawberry blancmange on a skateboard.*

What's pink and wobbly and has eight wheels?
*A bowl of strawberry blancmange on roller skates.*

What's pink and wobbly inside and white outside?
*A strawberry blancmange sandwich.*

What's pink and wobbly and croaks?
*A bowl of strawberry blancmange with a cold.*

Why don't strawberries play football?
*Have you ever seen a strawberry wearing football boots?*

What's pink and wobbly and shocking?
*Electric strawberry blancmange.*

**What do you get if you cross a sheep, a dog and a bowl of strawberry blancmange?**
*Collie-wobbles.*

**How can you tell a strawberry from an elephant?**
*A strawberry always forgets.*

**Why do strawberries always forget?**
*What have they got to remember?*

How do you keep a strawberry from ripening in August?
*Pick it in July.*

When does a strawberry wear a yellow shirt?
*When its red one is in the laundry.*

What's red and juicy and goes round and round?
*A long-playing strawberry.*

What do you call a two ton strawberry with a nasty temper?
*Sir!*

What do lady strawberries wear for tights?
*Garden hose.*

What's pink and wobbly and goes round and round?
*A bowl of blancmange in a revolving door.*

CUSTOMER: Why has my bowl of pink blancmange got footprints in it?

WAITER: Well, you said "Fetch me a bowl of pink blancmange, and step on it."

What's pink and wobbly on top, has four legs and a tail, and whinnies?

*A bowl of blancmange on a horse.*

What is the best thing to put into
strawberry pie?
*Your teeth!*

How can you tell a strawberry from
an aspirin?
*Strawberries don't come in bottles.*

Why don't strawberries have
dandruff?
*Did you ever see a strawberry with hair?*

What's red, washable, dries quickly
and needs no ironing?
*A drip-dry strawberry.*

What's red and goes at 60mph?
*A strawberry on a motorbike.*

What's red and comes off the ground
at 200mph?
*A jet-propelled strawberry.*

What's red and grows in an apple tree?
*A stupid strawberry.*

How do you stop a herd of
strawberries from charging?
*Take away their credit cards.*

What's red and goes "Beep! Beep!"?
*A strawberry in a traffic jam.*

What is red and highly dangerous?
*A herd of stampeding strawberries.*

Where was the first strawberry found?
*In a strawberry bed.*

What's big and red and lives in Scotland?
*The Loch Ness Strawberry.*

What's red and good at sums?
*A strawberry with a calculator.*

What's red and 440 metres high?
*The Empire State Strawberry.*

What's red and wears a mask?
*The Lone Strawberry.*

What's the best time to pick
strawberries?
*When the farmer is asleep.*

What's red and wobbles in the sky?
*A jelly-copter.*

What's red and wobbles, and fights
crime?
*Jelly Savalas.*

How do you start a jelly race?
*Say: "Get set."*

What's red and wobbles in a pram?
*A jelly-baby.*

What do jelly–babies wear on their feet?
*Gum-boots.*

What's red and wobbles in the corner of your living room?
*Jelly-vision.*

What's red and wobbles on the top of spongecake and custard in the middle of Paris?
*The Trifle Tower.*

"Waiter, what's the meaning of this dead fly in my strawberry blancmange?"
"I don't know sir, I don't tell fortunes."

"Waiter, waiter, there's a fly in my strawberry blancmange!"
"Would you prefer it to be served separately?"

"Waiter, waiter, there's a fly in my strawberry blancmange!"
"Yes sir, the chef used to be a tailor."

How many cabbages can you put in an empty sack?
*One – after that, the sack isn't empty.*

Why didn't the boy eat his spinach after his mother told him it would put colour in his cheeks?
*He didn't want green cheeks.*

What do you call a vegetable's wages?
*His celery.*

Why did the farmer run a steamroller over his potato patch?
*Because he wanted mashed potatoes.*

TEACHER (on school dinner duty): Any complaints?
PUPIL: Yes sir, these peas are too hard.
TEACHER (taking a spoonful and tasting them): They seem soft enough to me.
PUPIL: They are now. I've been chewing them for the last half hour.

CUSTOMER: Have you got any asparagus?
WAITER: No, we don't serve sparrows, and my name is *not* Gus.

What is the poorest plant?
A *vine, because it cannot support itself.*

What's green, lives in a pod, and is
a Kung Fu expert?
*Bruce Pea.*

What do you get if you cross
rabbits with leeks?
*Bunions.*

How do you make jumping beans?
*Get some beans, go up behind
them, and shout "Boo!"*

What do you call two turnips who
fall in love?
*Swedehearts.*

What is green, curly, and religious?
*Lettuce pray.*

Why was the farmer cross?
*Because someone trod on his corn.*

Knock, knock.
– Who's there?
Artichoke.
– Artichoke who?
Artichoke when he swallowed
strawberry blancmange.

Knock, knock.
– Who's there?
Worzel.
– Worzel who?
It's upstairs – first on the left.

Knock, knock.
– Who's there?
Beets.
– Beets who?
Beets me, but I just forgot the joke.

Knock, knock.
– Who's there?
Turnip.
– Turnip who?
Turnip for work at nine or you're fired!

Knock, knock.
– Who's there?
Lettuce.
– Lettuce who?
Lettuce tell you a few good pink and wobbly jokes!

Knock, knock.
– Who's there?
Bean.
– Bean who?
Bean working hard lately.

What is a mushroom?
*A place where Eskimoes train their huskies.*

Which town makes terrible sandwiches?
*Oldham.*

What's the best thing to eat with a
jacket potato?
*Button mushrooms.*

*Knock, knock.*
*– Who's there?*
*Strawberry.*
*– Strawberry who?*
*Knock, knock.*
*– Who's there?*
*Strawberry.*
*Strawberry who?*

What's white on the outside and
tells terrible jokes?
*A corny beef sandwich.*

Knock, knock.
– Who's there?
Orange.
Orange who?
Orange you glad I didn't say strawberry!

Why do toadstools grow close
together?
*Because they don't need mushroom.*

What's white on the outside and
acts badly?
*A ham sandwich.*

What's white outside, grey and slimy inside, and moves very slowly?
*A slug sandwich.*

What's white on the outside, pink inside, and talks to itself?
*A tongue sandwich.*

What's white on the outside, grey inside, and heavy on your stomach?
*An elephant sandwich.*

What grows in gardens, makes a sandwich, and is dangerous if you run into it?
*A hambush.*

What's pink and fills policemen's sandwiches?
*Truncheon meat.*

What's white on the outside and
scares easily?
*A chicken sandwich.*

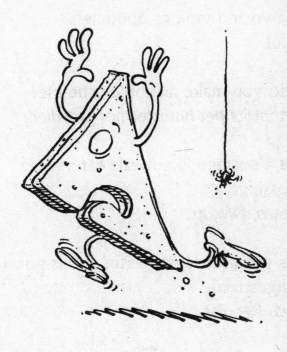

What's the best way to start a
pudding race?
*Sago.*

What's 300 metres tall, weighs 7,620
tonnes, and is made of jelly?
*The Trifle Tower.*

What do you call a three-barrelled rifle?
*A trifle.*

What's the difference between
frogspawn and tapioca pudding?
*Not a lot.*

How do you make an apple crumble?
*Tell it that its pet hamster has just died.*

Why is a cottage like meals eaten on a
sea crossing?
*Two down, two up.*

What's got four legs, glasses and is good
for indigestion?
*The Two Rennies.*

What's the best way of stopping
sea sickness?
*Bolt your food down.*

Why don't the Chinese eat custard?
*Have you ever tried eating custard with
chopsticks?*

What's a sick joke?
*Something that shouldn't be brought up in conversation.*

What's yellow and smells of bananas?
*Monkey sick.*

"Doctor, doctor, my tongue is as yellow as custard, my legs feel like jelly."
"Don't worry, you're just a trifle ill."

What kind of salad speaks for itself?
*Tongue salad.*

"What's the difference between a five pound note and a lettuce?"
"I don't know."
"You couldn't lend me a lettuce, could you?"

What did the mayonnaise say to the fridge?
*"Shut the door, I'm dressing."*

What's green and served hot from the oven?
*An Irish salad.*

What did the tomato say to the cucumber under the mistletoe?
*"Lettuce alone."*

How do you know a sausage doesn't like being fried?
*Because it spits.*

What came after the Stone Age and
the Bronze Age?
*The Saus-Age.*

The sausage is a cunning bird
With feathers long and wavy;
It swims about the frying pan
And makes its nest in gravy.

What car is like a sausage?
*An old banger.*

How do you make a sausage roll?
*Push it.*

**What's blue and chewed by whales?**
*Blubber gum.*

**What's huge, icy and tastes delicious?**
*A glacier mint.*

A girl in a sweetshop is one and a half metres tall and wears size four shoes. What does she weigh?
*Sweets.*

What happened to the man who dreamed he was eating a giant marshmallow?
*He woke up to find his pillow had disappeared.*

What mint can't be eaten?
*The Royal Mint.*

What's round, tasty and lifts weights?
*An extra strong mint.*

What do ghosts chew?
*Booble gum.*

What do you get if you cross
bubblegum with a yo-yo?
*I don't know, but if you swallow it
by mistake it comes back up.*

"Doctor, doctor, my brother thinks
he's a piece of chewing gum."
"Well send him to see me."
"I can't, he's stuck under the
table."

What's JR's favourite sweet?
*Ewing gum.*

What sweets do idiots like best?
*Wally mixtures.*

Who was the Wild West sheriff who
lived on pickled onions?
*Wyatt Burp.*

What's white, round and giggles?
*A tickled onion.*

What's white, round and jumps
around the garden?
*A spring onion.*

What's green, spicy and pecks trees?
*Woody Woodpickle.*

What's a hedgehog's favourite lunch?
*Prickled onions.*

What's green, sour and cleans teeth?
*A tooth pickle.*

What's green, wears a black cloak and
holds up stage coaches?
*Dick Gherkin.*

What did the cucumber say to the jam
jar?
*"If you'd kept your mouth shut I wouldn't
be in this pickle."*

"Doctor, doctor, for the last ten years my brother has believed he is a hen."
"Goodness gracious, why didn't you come to me sooner?"
"We needed the eggs."

"Doctor, doctor, my mother thinks I'm crazy because I prefer pink socks to grey ones."
"What's crazy about that? So do I."
"Really? How do you like them – fried or boiled?"

"Doctor, doctor, I feel like a strawberry."
"So do I – get me one too."

"Doctor, doctor, this banana diet isn't working on me."
"Stop scratching and come down from the curtains."

"Doctor, doctor, can you give me something for my liver?"
"How about a pound of onions?"

Doctor: I'm afraid you've only got three minutes to live.
Patient: Is there nothing you can do for me?
Doctor: I could boil you an egg . . .

"Doctor, my family think I'm
mad."
"Why?"
"Because I like sausages."
"Nonsense, I like sausages too."
"You do? You must come round
and see my collection. I've got
hundreds."

"Doctor, doctor, I keep thinking
I'm a strawberry."
"Hmmm. You're really in a jam,
aren't you?"

A man went to the doctor complaining he was not feeling very well. "What do you eat?" the doctor asked. "I eat only snooker balls," came the reply. "Snooker balls?" "Yes, I have yellow and red balls for breakfast, black and brown balls for lunch, and pink and blue balls for dinner." "Ah, now I know what your trouble is," said the doctor. "You're not eating your greens."

Knock, knock.
– Who's there?
Marmalade.
– Marmalade who?
Marmalade me a little egg.

Knock, knock.
– Who's there?
Turnip.
– Turnip who?
Turnip this little lane, that's where I live.

Knock, knock.
– Who's there?
Jupiter.
– Jupiter who?
Jupiter fly in my soup?

Knock, knock.
– Who's there?
Stew.
– Stew who?
Stew late to ask questions.

Knock, knock.
– Who's there?
Four eggs.
– Four eggs who?
Four eggs ample.

Knock, knock.
– Who's there?
Tina.
– Tina who?
Tina pilchards.

Knock, knock.
– Who's there?
Halibut.
– Halibut who?
Halibut letting me in on the secret?

Knock, knock.
– Who's there?
Ketchup.
– Ketchup who?
Ketchup with me and I'll tell you.

Knock, knock.
– Who's there?
Pecan.
– Pecan who?
Pecan somebody your own size.

Knock, knock.
– Who's there?
Spook.
– Spook who?
Spook-etti.

Knock, knock.
– Who's there?
Cook.
– Cook who?
Cuckoo yourself! I didn't come here to
be insulted.

Knock, knock.
– Who's there?
Ice cream.
– Ice cream who?
Ice cream and scream and scream until
I'm sick.

Knock, knock.
– Who's there?
Kipper.
– Kipper who?
Kipper hands to yourself.

Knock, knock.
– Who's there?
Tuna.
– Tuna who?
Tuna violin and it will sound better.

Knock, knock.
– Who's there?
Doughnut.
– Doughnut who?
Doughnut let anyone else in but me.

Knock, knock.
– Who's there?
Roland.
– Roland who?
Roland butter please.

Knock, knock.
– Who's there?
Watson.
– Watson who?
Watson the menu today?

Knock, knock.
– Who's there?
Egbert.
– Egbert who?
Egbert no bacon.

Knock, knock.
– Who's there?
Alec.
– Alec who?
Alec coffee but I don't like tea.

Knock, knock.
– Who's there?
Irish stew.
– Irish stew who?
Irish stew in the name of the law.

Knock, knock.
– Who's there?
Butter.
– Butter who?
Butter be quick, I need to go to the bathroom.

"Dad, do slugs taste nice?"
"Of course not – why do you ask?"
"Because you've just eaten one that was in your salad."

Did you hear about the wally who did bird impressions?
*He ate worms.*

"Doctor, doctor, I think I'm a dumpling."
"Now, now, don't get in a stew."

**Why do Eskimos eat candles?**
*For light refreshment.*

What's sweet and musical?
*I-sing sugar.*

What's the best way to get rid of excess fat?
*Divorce him.*

What did the Eskimo wife sing when her husband came home for dinner?.
*"Whale Meet Again . . ."*

What did the meat say when it was
about to be put on the skewer?
*"Oh spear me, spear me . . ."*

What is the best way to serve leftovers?
*To somebody else.*

What is the best way to stop rice
sticking together?
*Boil each grain separately.*

What did the frankfurter say to
the ketchup?
*"That's enough of your sauce."*

What's hot and
goes "Hoot, hoot"?
*Kentucky
Fried Owl.*

**What's a hungry mathematician's food?**
*Anything, as long as it's a square meal.*

**What's yellow and deadly?**
*Chop sueycide.*

**What stays hot in the fridge?**
*Mustard.*

**What's meaty, boney and stands at an angle?**
*Lean chops.*

**What's small, blue and eats cakes?**
*A blue dwarf cake-eater.*

**What's sweet, sour, dangerous and travels?**
*Takeaway kung food.*

**What was Anne Boleyn's last meal?**
*Cold chops.*

What's brown, round and travels at 1,000mph?
*An intercontinental ballistic rissole.*

What's made of pastry and is good in emergencies?
*The quiche of life.*

What's wrapped in tin foil and has an on/off switch?
*A TV dinner.*

What tree has the best food?
*A pantry.*

Who needs to eat a balanced diet?
*A tightrope walker.*

When is a red-headed idiot like a biscuit?
*When he's a ginger nut.*

What's black and white and comes out
of the oven spitting mad?
*A hot cross nun.*

What's doughy and 50 metres high?
*The Leaning Tower of Pizza.*

What's white one minute and
brown the next?
*A white rat in a microwave.*

What's brown one minute and
white the next?
*A brown rat in the deep freeze.*

What do you get if you cross a cow
with a pile of money?
*Rich milk.*

What do you get if you cross a cow
with an Arab?
*A milk sheik.*

**What swims and gives milk?**
*A milk float.*

**What do you get if you cross a cow with a camel?**
*Lumpy milkshakes.*

**What's the best way to stop milk going sour?**
*Drink it when it's fresh.*

TEACHER: Name me four things with milk in them.
PUPIL: Coffee, tea, and two cows.

1ST CAT: How did you get on in the milk-drinking contest?
2ND CAT: I won by six laps.

What turns without moving?
*Milk – when it turns sour.*

What do you get if you cross a
chicken with an octopus?
*A Sunday dinner where everybody gets a
leg.*

What do you get if you cross a
chicken with a banjo?
*A self-plucking chicken.*

What do you get if you cross a hen with
a tongue and a hand?
*A finger-lickin' chicken.*

What do you get if you cross a pig with a flea?
*Pork scratchings.*

What do you call a man with beef, gravy and vegetables on his head?
*Stew.*

What do you get if you cross a pig with an elephant?
*Large pork chops.*

TEACHER: What is the climate like in New Zealand?
PUPIL: Very, very cold.
TEACHER: What makes you say that?
PUPIL: Well, when they send us meat it always arrives frozen.

How do you know when you're eating rabbit stew?
*When it's got hares in it.*

What do you get if you cross a five pound note with a refrigerator?
*Iced lolly.*

What do you get if you cross a
football team with an ice cream?
*Aston Vanilla.*

What do you get if you cross an
idiot with a fridge?
*An iced wally.*

Why did the ice cream cry?
*Because its mother had been a
wafer so long.*

What's cold, Israeli and sells ice
cream?
*Walls of Jericho.*

What's the best way of making a
dead dog float?
*Take a scoop of dead dog and a
scoop of ice cream . . .*

What's the difference between an ice
cream and a bully?
*You lick one, the other licks you.*

What weighs half a ton, travels at
70mph and drips?
*An articulated lolly.*

What's orange and comes out of the
ground at 150mph?
*An E-Type carrot.*

What's yellow and fills fields with music?
*Popcorn.*

What's green and camps?
*A boy sprout.*

What happened when the carrot died?
*There was a huge turnip at the funeral.*

What do you get if the world runs out of olive oil?
*Rusty olives.*

What's cold and comes in tins?
*Chilli beans.*

What's black, sweet and makes history lessons interesting?
*Dates.*

What was Noah's job?
*Preserving pears.*

What stands on one leg and has its heart on its head?
*A cabbage.*

If there are two tomatoes on horseback, which one is the cowboy?
*Neither – they're both redskins.*

What's green, weighs a ton, and can float in a glass of Martini?
*An olivephant.*

What's green and for hire?
*A taxi cabbage.*

What are two rows of cabbages
called?
*A dual cabbageway.*

What's green and sings?
*Elvis Parsley.*

What's white on the outside, green
on the inside and jumps?
*A frog sandwich.*

What do you fry French food in?
*Oo-la-lard.*

Who invented spaghetti?
*Someone using his noodle.*

What's the most frightening thing in
a Scottish restaurant?
*A man eating haggis.*

What happened when the abominable
snowman ate a curry?
*He melted.*

What's smelly and spoken in
Scotland?
*Garlic.*

How do people eat cheese in Wales?
*Caerphilly.*

What do you get if you cross a sandwich with a Parisian cathedral?
*The lunchpack of Notre Dame.*

What do you get if you cross a Scotsman with yellow dessert?
*Tartan custard.*

What do you call a Welsh biscuit?
*Dai Gestive.*

What do you call a Welsh apple?
*Taffy apple.*

Where would you find exploding spaghetti?
*In the Minestrone of Defence.*

What's a chicken's favourite cake?
*A layer cake.*

What's a lawyer's favourite pudding?
*Sue-it.*

What is a viper's favourite food?
*Hiss fingers.*

What's an astronaut's favourite
meal?
*Launch.*

What is a frog's favourite drink?
*Croaka Cola.*

# THE PURPLE AND SPOTTY JOKE BOOK

What's purple and spotty?
*A plum with measles.*

Why do plums always forget?
*What do they have to remember?*

What's purple and spotty and drinks from the wrong side of the glass?
*A plum with measles and hiccups.*

What do you call a plum that is green and skinny at harvest time?
*A failure.*

What's purple and spotty and coughs?
*A plum with measles and a bad chest.*

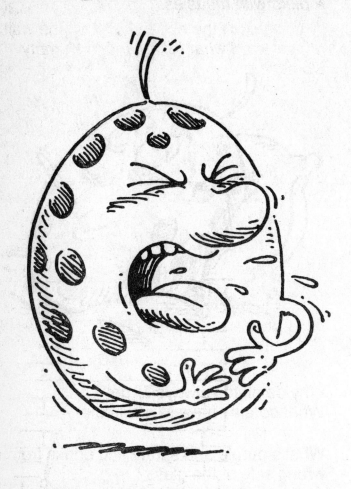

How were Humpty Dumpty and the plum with
a weak stem alike?
*They both had a great fall.*

What do you get if you cross two plums with a banana skin?
*A pair of purple slippers.*

Why wouldn't the ripe plum sit on the wall?
*It had heard what happened to Humpty Dumpty.*

What do you have when 2,000 plums try to get through a door together?
*Plum jam.*

What's purple and spotty and goes bang?
*A plum with measles in a minefield.*

What's purple and spotty and takes aspirins?
*A plum with measles and a headache.*

What does a plum do when it's raining?
*Gets wet.*

Why did the girl plum dye her hair yellow?
*To see if blondes have more fun.*


How can you tell a plum from an elephant?
*A plum always forgets.*

What did the plum say to the greenfly?
*You really bug me.*


What's the difference between a plum and a worm?
*Ever tried eating worm pie?*

What do you get if you cross a plum with an elephant?
*Fruit that never forgets.*

What do you get if you cross the M1 with a plum?
*Run over!*

What's a good way of putting on weight?
*Eat a plum, swallow the centre, and you've gained a stone.*

What family does the plum belong to?
*I don't know, nobody in our street has one.*

What did the Ribena say to the water?
*Diluted to meet you.*

Knock knock.
*Who's there?*
Orange.
*Orange who?*
Orange you glad I didn't say plum!

BOY: This Ribena is terrible.
FATHER: I made it in my pyjamas.
BOY: No wonder it tastes so bad.

What do you get if you cross a plum with an alligator?
*Fruit that bites back.*

What sort of tea makes you feel brave?
*Safety.*

What do you call a man who can sing and drink lemonade at the same time?
*A pop singer.*

What do you get if you cross a bottle of lemonade with Orville?
*Duck's Fizz.*

How do you make ginger wine?
*Twist his arm up his back.*

What did one chick say to the other chick
when it found an orange in the nest?
*Look at the orange mama laid!*

What do you get if you cross an orange with
a bell?
*An orange that can peal itself.*

Why did the orange go to the doctor?
*Because it wasn't peeling well.*

What's wet and comes out of a bottle at
100mph?
*An Aston Martini.*

Knock knock.
*Who's there?*
Plum.
*Plum who?*
Knock knock.
*Who's there?*
Plum.
*Plum who?*
Knock knock.
*Who's there?*
Plum.
*Plum who???*
Knock knock.
*Who's there?*
Orange.
*Orange who?*
Orange you glad I didn't

say plum!

How is a plum like a wise man?
*Neither reads the* Sun.

What did the green plum say to the blue plum?
*Cheer up!*

What do you get if you cross a bottle of
lemonade with a masseur?
*A fizzy o'therapist.*

What do little devils drink?
*Demonade.*

What did the orange say to the other orange
on the telephone?
*Nothing, the pips went!*

What do you do with a hurt lemon?
*Give it lemonade.*

Why couldn't the orange get up the hill?
*Because it had run out of juice.*

What does a vegetarian vampire eat?
*Blood oranges.*


What do you get when you cross an orange
and a squash court?
*Orange squash.*


What is square and green?
*A lemon in disguise.*

What was the orange doing in a palm tree?
*It had heard that coconuts have more fun.*


What is the difference between a lemon and
a melon?
*The order in which their letters are written.*

What is a tangerine?
*An orange in an easy-open wrapper.*

What's purple and highly dangerous?
*Shark-infested Ribena.*

Where do the world's biggest plums come
from?
*The world's biggest plum trees.*

What's purple on top, has four legs and a
tail, and whinnies?
*A plum on horseback.*

What is the best way to keep plums?
*Don't return them.*

What did one plum say to the other plum?
*Nothing. Plums can't talk.*

Who is purple, rides a motorbike, and jumps
over buses?
*Evel Plumevel.*

What was the smallest plum?
*Tom Plum.*

What did the dentist say when his wife baked
a plum pie?
*Can I do the filling?*

Why is a Boy Scout like a tin of plums?
*They are both prepared.*

Where do you find wild plums?
*It depends where they were lost.*

What's red and clings to metal?
*A magnetic tomato.*

If your cat ate an unripe plum, what would she become?
*A sourpuss.*

What's round, red and cheeky?
*Tomato sauce.*

What can a whole red tomato do but half a red tomato can't?
*Look round.*

What's purple and spotty and wears sunglasses?
*A plum with measles and a black eye.*

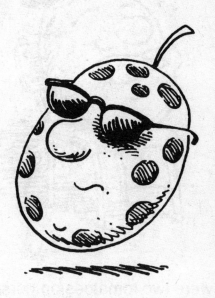

Why did the tomato go red?
*Because it saw the salad dressing.*

Why was the tomato in such a hurry?
*It wanted to ketchup (catch up).*

Why does a plum make a good museum keeper?
*Plum preserves.*

There were two tomatoes on horseback.
Which was the cowboy?
*Neither – they were both redskins.*

Why did the man have to go to hospital after the blackcurrant jam fell on his head?
*It was in a jar.*

A man saw a gardener pushing a wheel-barrow full of manure.
'Where are you going with that?' he asked.
'Going to put it on my blackcurrants,' said the gardener.
'Suit yourself,' said the man. 'I usually put sugar and cream on mine!'

1ST GIRL: Here, try some of this blackcurrant jam I've just made.
*2ND GIRL: Ugh! It's horrible!*
1ST GIRL: You've no taste – it definitely says in my cookery book that this recipe is delicious.

What should you do if your pet plum falls ill?
*Call the plumber.*

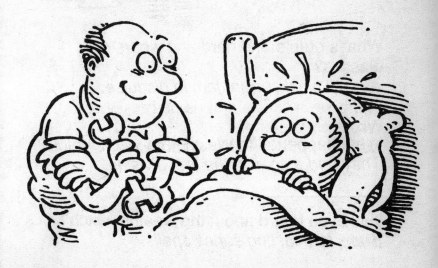

What's yellow on the outside and purple on the inside?
*A plum disguised as an apricot.*

What's purple and hard and wears dark glasses?
*A jar of blackcurrant jam in disguise.*


What happened to West Brom-witch Albion?
*They had a spell in the first division.*


Have you heard about the weather witch?
*She's forecasting sunny spells.*

What's purple and warty and smells?
*A witch's nose.*

What happens to a witch when she loses her temper?
*She flies off the handle.*

What's purple and hard and wears sunglasses?
*A jar of blackcurrant jam on holiday.*

What's purple and hard and moves along the bottom of the sea?
*A jar of blackcurrant jam in a submarine.*

What's purple and hard and has four wheels?
*A jar of blackcurrant jam on a skateboard.*

What's purple and hard and has eight wheels?
*A jar of blackcurrant jam on roller skates.*

Two witches came out of the theatre one night. One said to the other, 'Shall we walk home, or shall we take a broom?'

What happened to the naughty witch schoolgirl?
*She was ex-spelled.*

Why do witches get good bargains?
*Because they like to haggle.*

What are baby witches called?
*Halloweenies.*

What do you call two witches who share a broom?
*Broom-mates.*

What's the best thing to do with a green alien?
*Wait until he's ripe.*

What's purple and slimy and goes up and down?
*An alien in a lift.*


What has three purple eyes like an alien, an arm like an alien, four hands like an alien, but isn't an alien?
*A photograph of an alien.*


What happens if you are confronted with two identical hags?
*You can't tell witch is witch.*

Why did the witch put her broom in the washing machine?
*She wanted a clean sweep.*

LITTLE BOY TO PARROT IN ZOO: Say little birdie, can you talk?
*PARROT: Yes, can you fly?*

What do you get if you cross a parrot with a homing pigeon?
*A bird that asks its way home if it gets lost.*

Why can't you find aspirins in the jungle?
*Because the parrots eat 'em all!*

What did the astronaut say about the ten-legged aliens?
*Don't worry, they're armless.*

ALIEN TO HIS FRIEND: What's that ugly purple thing on your neck? Oh sorry, it's your head!

What do you get if you cross a parrot with a soldier?
*A parrot-trooper.*

What's purple and slimy and travels at
100mph?
*An alien on a motorbike.*

What singing birds come from Cornwall?
*The Parrots of Penzance.*

Did you hear about the scientist who crossed
a parrot with a crocodile?
*It bit off his arm and said, 'Who's a pretty boy
then?'*

TEACHER: What is a polygon?
*PUPIL: An empty parrot cage, Miss.*

A purple and slimy alien was travelling by himself in his spaceship. As he hovered over a farm, he called down to the farmer: 'Hallo, Earthling. Where am I?' The farmer looked up. 'You can't fool me,' he shouted. 'You're up there in that little spaceship!'

What happens when aliens hold a beauty
contest?
*Nobody wins.*

Who is safe when a man-eating leopard is
loose?
*Women and children.*

Where do you find leopards?
*It depends where you lost them.*

Who would win a fight between an African lion and an African tiger?
*Neither – there aren't any tigers in Africa.*

When should you feed leopard's milk to a baby?
*When it's a baby leopard.*

Did you hear about the man who bought his mother a very rare parrot for her birthday? It could speak ten languages, play chess, and sing the entire works of Mozart. He asked her what she thought of the bird.
'It was delicious, son,' she said, 'absolutely delicious . . .'

When is a man-eating leopard most likely to enter your house?
*When the door is open.*

What do you get if you cross a plum with a leopard?
*A highly dangerous purple people-eater.*

What do you stuff dead parrots with?
*Polyfilla.*

What do you get if you cross a fierce leopard with Father Christmas?
*Santa Claws.*

A leopard was about to eat a missionary. It had the man cornered, but suddenly fell down on its knees and started to pray.
'It's a miracle!' cried the missionary. 'I'm saved! The tiger isn't going to eat me after all.'
Just then, a heavenly voice boomed down. 'You're wrong,' it said, 'he *is* going to eat you. But first, he's saying his grace.'

What is a Macaw?
*A Scottish parrot.*

Why shouldn't you pull a leopard by his tail?
*It may only be his tail, but it could be your end.*

What did the idiot call his pet tiger?
*Spot!*

ZOOKEEPER: I've just crossed a hyena with a leopard.
*ASSISTANT: What did you get?*
ZOOKEEPER: I don't know, but when it laughs you'd better join in.

What do French people eat for breakfast?
*Huit heures bix!*

What's purple and French and writes under
an assumed name?
*Nom de plum.*

What would you get if all the cars in France
were purple?
*A purple carnation.*

What do you get if you cross the Channel
with a sailing ship?
*To the other side.*

What's a guillotine?
*A French chopping centre.*

What's 300 metres tall, weighs 7,620 tons
and attracts bees?
*The Eiffel Flower.*

What's wrapped in cling-film and terrorises Paris?
*The lunch-pack of Notre Dame.*


What's the quickest way to the Gard du Nord station?
*Run as fast as you can.*


What's purple and spotty?
*A grape that eats too much chocolate.*

What's made of chocolate and rolls along the seabed?
*An oyster egg.*

What's woolly, covered in chocolate, and floats around the sun?
*A Mars baaa.*

What's clever, made of chocolate and travels by underground?
*A Tube of Smarties.*

What did the chocolate say to the lollipop?
*Hi, sucker.*

What do you call a girl that's covered in chocolate?
*Candy.*

What do you get if you cross an elk with a packet of cocoa?
*Chocolate moose.*

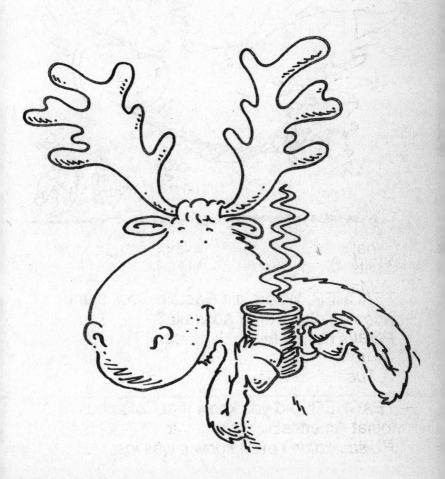

What's purple and yellow and green, with a twenty-metre wingspan?
*A two-ton parrot.*

TEACHER: Where did Captain Cook stand when he discovered Australia?
*PUPIL: On his feet.*

TEACHER: Did you know that Columbus found America?
*PUPIL: I didn't even know it was lost.*

What do you get if you cross a chocolate with a madman?
*A coconut.*

Who was purple and discovered America in 1492?
*Christopher Plumbus.*

Who sailed around Ireland and invented mints?
*Marc O'Polo.*

TEACHER: On what date did Columbus cross the Atlantic?
*PUPIL: He didn't cross on a date, he crossed on a ship.*

What did the cannibal say when he met the famous explorer?
*Doctor Livingstone, I consume?*

What do you get if you cross eight arms with a watch?
*A clocktopus.*

What's wet and says 'How do you do?' sixteen times?
*Two octopuses shaking hands.*

What makes an octopus a very good fighter?
*He is well-armed.*

What bus sailed the ocean?
*Columbus.*

Which ghost discovered America?
*Christopher Ghoulumbus.*

What lives under the sea and carries 64 people?
*An octobus.*

Who snatched the baby octopus and held it to ransom?
*Squidnappers.*

Why did the man cross a chicken with an octopus?
*So his family could have a leg each.*

Who was round and purple and ruled Russia?
*Peter the Grape.*

What's purple and has eight legs?
*An octoplum.*

IGOR: Why is Baron Frankenstein such
good fun?
MONSTER: *Because he soon has you
in stitches!*

Why was Baron Frankenstein never lonely?
*Because he was good at making friends.*

What do you call a neurotic octopus?
*A crazy mixed-up squid.*

1ST MONSTER: The bride of Frankenstein has a lovely face.
*2ND MONSTER: If you can read between the lines.*

What did Frankenstein's monster say when he was struck by lightning?
*Great! That was just what I needed.*

Did you hear what happened to
Frankenstein's monster?
*He was stopped for speeding, fined £50, and
dismantled for six months.*

Who is purple, has scars on his head, and
frightens people?
*Frankenplum.*

What do you call a clever monster?
*Frank Einstein.*

What does Frankenstein's monster call a
screwdriver?
*Daddy.*

What is written on the grave of
Frankenstein's monster?
*Rust in peace.*

Who brings the monsters their babies?
*Frankenstork.*

How did Frankenstein's monster eat his lunch?
*He bolted it down.*

Who conquered half the world, laying eggs along the way?
*Attila the Hen.*

Where did the Vikings drink?
*At Norse troughs.*

Who led hordes of fighting convent girls?
*Attila the Nun.*

Who was Russia's greatest gardener?
*Ivan-hoe!*

Who was full of hay and conquered
Mongolia?
*Ghengis Barn.*

A diner in a restaurant asked the waitress what flavours of ice cream were on the menu. The waitress answered in a very hoarse whisper: 'Vanilla, chocolate, and blackcurrant.' Sympathising with her condition, the man asked: 'Do you have laryngitis?' 'No,' croaked the waitress, 'just the vanilla, chocolate and blackcurrant.'

What do you get if you cross an invader with a cake?
*Attila the Bun.*

How did the Vikings communicate with each other?
*By Norse code.*

Which cyclist defeated the Spanish Armada?
*Sir Francis Trike.*

Two ants were in a supermarket. They climbed up on a shelf and on to a box containing a blackcurrant pie. Suddenly the first ant began running.

'Wait for me', cried the other ant.

'What's the hurry?'

'Can't you read?' said the first. 'It says here: TEAR ALONG THE DOTTED LINE.'

What's purple and wobbles in the sky?
*A blackcurrant jelly-copter.*

**MAN IN RESTAURANT:** Will you join me in a piece of blackcurrant pie?
*WOMAN: Do you think there's room for both of us?*

Why did the blackberry jelly wobble?
*Because it saw the milk shake.*

What's big and wobbly, and fights crime?
*Jelly Savalas.*

What's small and wobbly and sits in a pram?
*A jelly-baby.*

Why are blackcurrant seeds like gateposts?
*Because they propagate.*


What is purple, has one bionic eye, and
fights crime?
*The Six Million Dollar Aubergine.*


How many aubergines can you put into an
empty sack?
*One. After that the sack is no longer empty.*


What's purple and wobbles in the corner of
your living-room?
*A blackcurrant jelly-vision.*

What wobbles on a pile of blancmange in the middle of Paris?
*The Trifle Tower.*


What are you if you've got a blancmange in one ear, and a jelly in the other?
*A trifle deaf.*

What did one aubergine say to the other aubergine?
*Take me to your weeder.*


What is purple and goes putt, putt?
*An outboard aubergine.*

What's purple and comes out of the ground
at 100mph?
*An E-type aubergine.*

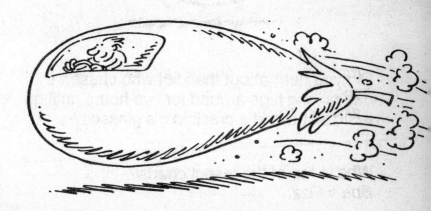

How do you tell the good aubergines from the bad ones?
*The good aubergines have haloes.*

Did you hear about the idiot who chased a daddy long legs around for two hours until he realized he had a crack in his glasses?

Who is top of the insect charts?
*Bug's Fizz.*

Why did the baby aubergine colour itself orange?
*So it could hide in the carrot patch.*


Knock, knock.
*Who's there?*
Weevil.
*Weevil who?*
Weevil work it out.


CUSTOMER: Waiter, there's a cockroach in my soup!
*WAITER: Yes sir, the fly is on holiday.*


What's purple and spotty and flies badly?
*A ladybird with a bruised back.*

What goes 99-klonk, 99-klonk, 99-klonk?
*A centipede with a wooden leg.*

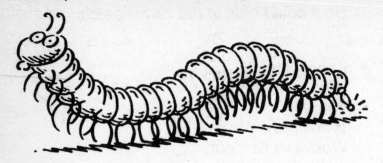

What is red, has bumps and a horse, and
lives on the prairie?
*The Lone Raspberry.*

What do you get when you cross an apple with a Christmas tree?
*A pineapple.*

What did one strawberry say to the other strawberry?
*Between you and me, we shouldn't be in this jam.*

Did you hear about the idiot caterpillar?
*It turned into a frog!*

Why did the baby strawberry cry?
*Because his mother was in a jam.*

What did the girl say after she ate a basket of fresh plums?
*Burp!*

What is rhubarb?
*Celery with high blood pressure.*

When insects take a trip, how do they travel?
*In a buggy.*

Which famous Norseman sailed the Atlantic
a thousand years ago?
*Eric the Red Apple.*

What do farmers do to endangered
strawberries?
*Put them in preserves.*


Did you hear the story about the world's
biggest strawberry?
*Never mind, it's over your head.*

Who was purple and burnt the cakes?
*Alfred the Grape.*

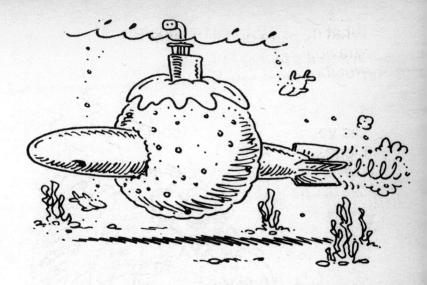

What's purple and steaming and travels
along the seabed?
*A plum pudding in a submarine.*


Why is plum pudding like the sea?
*Because it's full of currants.*


What's purple and steaming and goes up
and down?
*A plum pudding in a lift.*


What's purple and steaming and goes slam-
slam-slam-slam?
*A four-door plum pudding.*

When is plum pudding musical?
*When it's piping hot.*

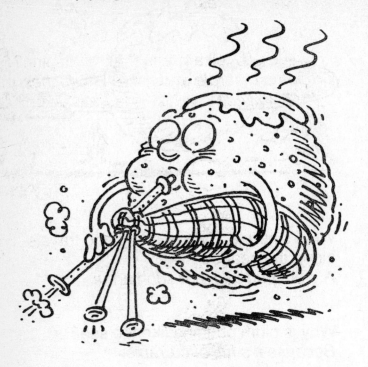

BOY: I don't like this plum pudding.
*WOMAN: Oh, don't you? I'll have you know I was making plum puddings before you were born.*
BOY: Perhaps this is one of them.

What is the best thing to put into plum pudding?
*Your teeth.*

What American lakes are filled with purple juice?
*The Grape Lakes.*


How can you tell a grape from an aspirin?
*Grapes are purple and come in bunches.*

MAN: This plum pudding is nice and warm.
*WOMAN: It should be – the cat's been sitting on it.*


What's purple, washable, dries quickly and needs no ironing?
*A drip-dry grape.*

Why don't grapes have dandruff?
*Did you ever see a grape with hair?*

Why didn't the grape snore?
*Because it was afraid of waking up the rest of the bunch.*

Why did the grape go to the doctor?
*Because it wasn't peeling very well?*

What's purple and round and floats in space?
*The Planet of the Grapes.*

Who was purple and ruled the world?
*Alexander the Grape.*

What did the grape say when the elephant trod on it?
*Nothing – it just gave out a little wine.*

What's purple and steaming and comes at you from all sides?
*Stereophonic plum pudding.*

What do you get if you cross an aubergine with a skunk?
*A skunk with a purple streak down its back.*

What's purple and goes 'Beep, beep'?
*An aubergine in a traffic jam.*

What was the film where 100 grapes tunnelled out of the prisoner-of-war camp?
*The Grape Escape.*

Why can't an aubergine be twelve inches long?
*Because then it would be a foot.*

Why don't aubergines worry when people say nasty things about them?
*Aubergines are noted for their thick skins.*

TEACHER: How do you spell 'aubergine'?
PUPIL: *O-b-e-r-j-e-a-n.*
TEACHER: The dictionary spells it a-u-b-e-r-g-i-n-e.
PUPIL: *You didn't ask me how the dictionary spells it!*

What's purple and good at sums?
*An aubergine with a calculator.*

TEACHER: If I had eight aubergines in one hand, and six in the other, what would I have?
PUPIL: Big hands.

What's long and purple and red all over?
An embarrassed aubergine.

SHERLOCK HOLMES: Ah, Watson, you are wearing your purple thermal underpants today . . .
DR WATSON: Absolutely astounding, Holmes! How on earth did you deduce that?
SHERLOCK HOLMES: Elementary, my dear Watson. You forgot to put your trousers on.

What's long and purple and goes 'hith'?
*A purple snake with a lisp.*

That's a strange pair of socks you've got on
– one dark purple and one light purple.
*I know – I've got another pair just like it at
home.*

What's big and purple and lives in Scotland?
*The Loch Ness Aubergine.*

What's purple and points north?
*A magnetic aubergine.*

What is an aubergine skin most used for?
*To keep the aubergine together.*


What's purple and points south?
*A stupid magnetic aubergine.*

What is purple and runs in slow motion?
*The Bionic Nose.*

What's purple and goes thump-squish, thump-squish?
*An aubergine with one wet plimsoll.*

Why don't they grow aubergines any longer?
*Because they're long enough already.*

How do you stop a herd of aubergines from charging?
*Take away their credit cards.*

What do purple cabbages use for stockings?
*Garden hose.*

What is the hardest thing to eat?
*An aubergine sideways.*

What's long and purple and roars around the
vegetable patch at 60mph?
*An aubergine on a motorbike.*

Why was the purple cabbage disliked by all
the other vegetables?
*It had a big head.*

What's purple and close to France?
*Grape Britain.*

How did the purple cabbage talk to the green cabbage?
*Head to head.*

How can you find the most attractive purple cabbage in the patch?
*She's the one with the most boyfriends.*

Why didn't the boy eat his purple cabbage after his mother told him it would put colour in his cheeks?
*He didn't want purple cheeks.*


Why are purple cabbages so generous?
*Because they have big hearts.*


What happened to the criminal prune?
*It was taken into custardy.*


What's purple and curly and jumps up and down?
*A purple cabbage at a disco.*

Where can you find aubergines, potatoes, broccoli and swedes, no matter what time of the year it is?
*In the dictionary.*

LADY (to a tramp who's asked for a meal): Do you like cold prunes and custard?
*TRAMP: I love it, lady.*
LADY: Well call back later, it's very hot right now.

How can you tell an apple from a purple cabbage?
*If it's red it's probably an apple.*

What's green and red and purple and spins round at 100mph?
*Kermit eating grapes in a liquidizer.*

Why did the police arrest the purple cabbage?
*It was involved in a garden plot.*

Why did the grape go out with the prune?
*Because he couldn't find a date.*

What do you get if you cross a grape with a comedian?
*Peels of laughter.*

What do you get if you cross a bowl of prunes and custard with a pair of roller skates?
*Meals on wheels.*

What's purple and lumpy and wears sunglasses?
*Prunes and custard on holiday.*

What's red outside, purple and yellow inside, and very crowded?
*A bus full of prunes and custard.*

What's purple and lumpy inside and white outside?
*A prunes and custard sandwich.*

What's purple, covered in custard, and miserable?
*Plum grumble.*

Why did the man have to go to hospital after the prune fell on his head?
*It was in a tin.*


What's purple and highly dangerous?
*A bunch of stampeding grapes.*


What's purple and glows in the dark?
*A 100 watt grape.*

What's purple and barks at people?
*A Grape Dane.*

Who swings through the vines?
*Tarzan of the Grapes.*

What's purple and lumpy and goes round and round?
*Prunes and custard in a revolving door.*

What's purple and highly dangerous?
*A bunch of angry grapes.*

If you have a referee in boxing, a referee in football, and a referee in rugby, what do you have in bowls?
*Prunes and custard.*

What's purple and 8,000 kilometres long?
*The Grape Wall of China.*

What's purple and ruled Russia?
*Catherine the Grape.*

What do you get when you cross a grape
with a chicken?
*A hen that lays bunches of purple eggs.*

What's purple has four wheels and is used in
wine making?
*Grapes – I lied about the wheels.*

What's green and hairy on the outside, and
purple on the inside?
*A grape disguised as a gooseberry.*

Why are grapes never lonely?
*Because they hang around in bushes.*

What's yellow and highly dangerous?

*A bunch of angry bananas.*

How do you stop a herd of bananas from charging?
*Take away their credit cards.*

What is yellow, has one bionic eye, and fights crime?
*The Six Million Dollar Banana.*

What is yellow, then green, then yellow, then green?
*A banana that works part-time as a cucumber.*

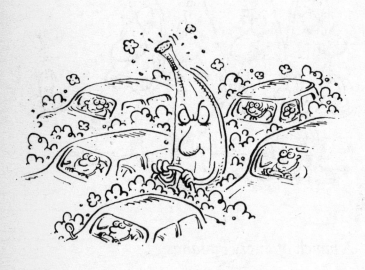

What's yellow and goes 'Beep! Beep!'?
*A banana in a traffic jam.*

What is made from two banana skins?
*A pair of slippers.*

What do you get if you cross two bananas
with a tomato?
*A pair of red slippers.*

What is the best thing to put into banana pie?
*Your teeth!*

How can you tell a banana from an aspirin?
*Bananas come in bunches.*

Why don't bananas have dandruff?
*Did you ever see a banana with hair?*

What's yellow, washable, dries quickly
and needs no ironing?
*A drip-dry banana.*


What's yellow and goes at 60mph?
*A banana on a motorbike.*

What's yellow and comes out of the
trees at 200mph?
*A jet-propelled banana.*

What's yellow and grows in an apple
tree?
*A stupid banana.*

What's yellow and has twenty-two legs?
*Banana United!*

Why don't they grow bananas any
longer?
*Because they're long enough already.*

What's yellow and hums?
*An electric banana.*

Knock, knock.
– *Who's there?*

Banana.
– *Banana who?*

Knock, knock.
– *Who's there?*

Banana.
– *Banana who?*

Knock, knock.
– *Who's there?*

Orange.
– *Orange who?*

Orange you glad I didn't say banana?

**What's yellow and goes round and round and round?**
*A banana in a washing machine.*

If a crocodile makes shoes, what does a banana make?
*Slippers.*

Why didn't the banana snore?
*Because it was afraid of waking up the rest of the bunch.*

Why did the strawberry jelly wobble?
*Because it saw the banana milk-shake.*

Why did the banana go to the doctor?
*Because it wasn't peeling very well.*

**What's yellow
and points
north?**
*A magnetic
banana.*

**What's yellow
and points
south?**
*A stupid
magnetic
banana.*

What's yellow and goes click-click?
*A ball-point banana*

What do you get if you cross a yellow
fruit with a bell?
*A banana that can peel itself.*

How do you stop a banana from
ripening on Sunday?
*Pick it on Saturday.*

What's yellow and goes
slam-slam-slam-slam?
*A four-door banana.*

What is a banana skin most used for?
*To keep the banana together.*

Why did the banana
go out with
the prune?
*Because he couldn't
find a date.*

What's yellow and goes up and down?
*A banana in a lift.*

What's yellow
and goes
thump-squish,
thump-squish?
*A banana with one wet plimsoll.*

What's enormous and yellow and says
'Fe-fi-fo-fum'?
*A giant banana.*

What's yellow, wears a cape, and fights
crime?
*Superbanana.*

What's yellow
and square?
*A banana in
disguise.*

What's yellow and 440 metres high?
*The Empire State Banana.*

What's yellow
and wears
a mask?
*The Lone Banana.*

What do you get if you cross a banana with a skunk?
*A skunk with a yellow streak down its back.*

What did the banana do when the chimpanzee chased it?
*The banana split.*

What do you get if you cross a banana with a comedian?
*Peels of laughter.*

What's the best time to pick bananas?
*When the farmer is in bed.*

Why are apples red?
*If they were yellow they'd be lemons.*

What do you get if you cross an apple with a Christmas tree?
*A pineapple.*

What's an apple that is small and yellow at picking time?
*A failure.*

What's red and miserable and covered in custard?
*Apple grumble.*

What is yellow and highly dangerous?
*A herd of stampeding bananas.*

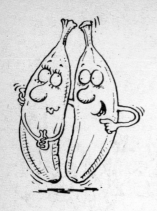

What did the
handsome boy
banana say
to the pretty
girl banana?
*'You appeal to me.'*

What's big and yellow and lives in
Scotland?
*The Loch Ness Banana.*

What's yellow and good at sums?
*A banana with a calculator.*

What's yellow, washable, and doesn't need ironing?
*A drip-dry banana.*

Why is a banana skin like a pullover?
*Because it's easy to slip on.*

Where was the first banana found?
*In a tree.*

What is worse than a redskin on the warpath?
*A banana skin on the footpath.*

What do you get if you cross a yellow fruit with a Greek singer?
*Banana Mouskouri.*

What is the hardest thing to eat?
*A banana sideways.*

What's yellow has four wheels and is eaten by monkeys?
*Bananas – I lied about the wheels.*

Why can't a banana be twelve inches long?
*Because then it would be a foot.*

**What would you do if you found a blue banana?**
*Try to cheer it up.*

**What do you get hanging from banana trees?**
*Aching arms.*

What's yellow and jumps up and down?
*A banana at a disco.*


What's long and yellow and shaped like a banana?
*A banana.*

What's long and yellow and says 'Pardon'?
*A polite banana with hiccups.*

'What's the difference between a £5 pound note and a banana?'
*'I don't know.'*
'You couldn't lend me a banana, could you?'

What do you
get if you
cross a rug
with a banana?
*A carpet slipper.*

What's the difference between stork and butter?
*Butter can't stand on one leg.*

What's the best butter in the world?
*A goat.*

**What's yellow and highly dangerous?**
*A canary with a machine-gun.*

**What's left after a lawn-mower runs over a canary?**
*Shredded Tweet.*

**What do you get if you cross a cat with a canary?**
*A satisfied cat and a dead canary.*

What do you get if you cross an elephant with a canary?
A very messy cage.

Man: This canary you sold me has a broken leg.
Pet shop owner: You only asked for a good singer – I didn't know you wanted him to dance as well.

Man: Can I have a canary for my wife please?
Pet shop owner: I'm sorry sir, we don't do swaps.

What succeeds like nothing else?
A toothless canary.

What bird cannot fly as high as you can jump?
A canary in a cage.

What do you do with sick canaries?
Give them tweetment.

What's yellow and has a wingspan of fifteen metres?
A two and a half ton canary.

What's yellow, has twenty-four legs, and sings?
Twelve canaries.

DEBBIE: I have a canary that can do something I can't.
EMMA: What's that?
DEBBIE: Take a bath in a teacup.

What's yellow and highly dangerous?
Chop sueycide

What's yellow and fills fields with music?
*Popcorn.*

What's small and furry and cuts corn?
*A combine hamster.*

What did the little corn say to momma corn?
'Where's popcorn?'

Why shouldn't
you tell secrets
in a vegetable garden?
Because corn has ears.

Why was the farmer hopping mad?
Because somebody stepped on his corn.

Where did the baby ear of corn come from?
The stalk brought him.

Why was the corn stalk angry with the farmer?
The farmer kept pulling its ears.


Why did the idiot put corn in his shoes?
Because of his pigeon toes.


Two ears of corn were running up a hill.
What were they when they got to the top?
Puffed wheat.

# Lemon

What's yellow
and goes round
and round and
round?
A long-playing
lemon.

What's yellow, full of seeds, and looks
like half a lemon?
The other half of the lemon.

What's yellow, sour, and goes 'Splutter, splutter, splutter'?
A lemon running out of juice.

What's cowardly, thin, and full of noodles?
Chicken soup.

What do you get if you cross a cowardly cow with a pullover?
A yellow jersey.

**What is yellow and highly dangerous?**
*Kamikaze custard.*

**What's yellow and prickly?**
*A cowardy custard hedgehog.*

What's the better fighter, a banana or
a chicken?
*A banana - it's no chicken.*

What happened to the criminal
banana?
*It was taken into custardy.*

What's yellow and stupid?
*Thick custard.*

Why do elephants paint their toe- nails
yellow?
*So they can hide upside down in
custard.*

How can you tell when there's an
elephant in your custard?
*When it's especially lumpy.*

If you have a referee in boxing, a
referee in football, and a referee in
rugby, what do you have in bowls?
*Custard.*

Lady to a tramp who's asked for a meal: *Do you like cold custard?*
Tramp: *I love it, lady.*
Lady: *Well call back later, it's very hot right now.*

What's yellow and wobbly and wears dark glasses?
*A bowl of custard in disguise.*

What happened to the man who couldn't tell putty from custard?
*His windows fell out.*

What's red outside, yellow inside, and very crowded?
*A bus of custard.*

Why did the man
have to go to
hospital after
the custard fell
on his head?
*It was in a tin.*

A man saw a gardener pushing a wheel-barrow full of manure. 'Where are you going with that?' he asked. *'Going to put it on my goosberries,'* said the gardener. 'Suit yourself,' said the man, 'I usually put custard on mine.'

What's yellow and wobbly
and comes at you
from all sides?
*Stereophonic custard.*

What's yellow and wobbly and goes round and round?
*A bowl of long-playing custard.*

What's yellow and wobbly and moves along the bottom of the sea?
*A bowl of custard in a submarine.*

Canteen lady: Do you want more of this custard?
Boy: *No thanks, I'm too young to die.*

Boy: Have you got any custard left?
Canteen lady: *Yes.*
Boy: Well you shouldn't have made so much then.

Boy: Can I have some custard please?
Canteen lady: *One lump or two?*

1st girl: Here, try some of this banana custard I've just made.
2nd girl: *Ugh! It's horrible!*
1st girl: You've no taste – it definitely says in my cookery book that this recipe is delicious.

What's yellow and wobbly and wears sunglasses?
*A bowl of custard on holiday.*

What's yellow and wobbly and has four wheels?
*A bowl of custard on a skateboard.*

What's yellow
and wobbly
and has eight
wheels?
*A bowl of
custard on
roller skates.*

What's yellow and wobbly and goes bang?
*A bowl of custard in a minefield.*


What's yellow and wobbly inside and white outside?
*A custard sandwich.*


What's yellow and wobbly and croaks?
*A bowl of custard with a cold.*


What do you get if you cross a sheep, a dog and a bowl of custard?
*Collie-wobbles.*


What's 300 metres tall, weighs 7,620 tons, and is made of custard?
*The Trifle Tower.*

What's yellow and highly dangerous?
*An Eggs-ocet missile.*

What is yellow and flat and goes around at 33 1/3 revolutions per minute?
*A long-playing omelette.*

What's yellow and white and travels at 100mph?
*A train-driver's egg sandwich.*

What do you get if you cross a hen with a poodle?
*Pooched eggs.*

What do you get if you cross a hen with an electric organ?
*Hammond eggs.*

Have you heard the one about the three boiled eggs?
*Two bad!*

Why did the egg go into the jungle?
*Because it was an egg-splorer.*

If an egg came floating down the River Thames, where would it have come from?
*A chicken.*

What's the best way to make an egg roll?
*Push it down a hill.*

What do you get if you cross a chicken with a kangaroo?
*Pouched eggs.*

Knock, knock.
— *Who's there?*
Egbert.
— *Egbert who?*
Egbert no bacon.

There were two eggs boiling in a saucepan. One said, 'Phew, it's hot in here.' The other egg said, *'Wait till you get out, you'll get your head bashed in.'*

What sort of food do fighter pilots prefer?
*Scrambled eggs.*

Knock, knock.
— *Who's there?*
Exam.
— *Exam who?*
Eggs, ham and cheese.

Who conquered half the world, laying eggs along the way?
Attila the Hen.

Doctor: I'm afraid you only have three more minutes to live.
Patient: Is there nothing you can do for me?
Doctor: I could boil you an egg.

'Waiter, these eggs are bad.'
Don't blame me, I only laid the table.'

What's a mischievous egg called?
A practical yolker.

What's the best way to make an egg
roll?
Push it downhill.

How do Daleks deal with eggs?
They eggs- terminate them.

What do you get if you give chickens
whisky?
Scotch eggs.

# What's yellow and highly dangerous?

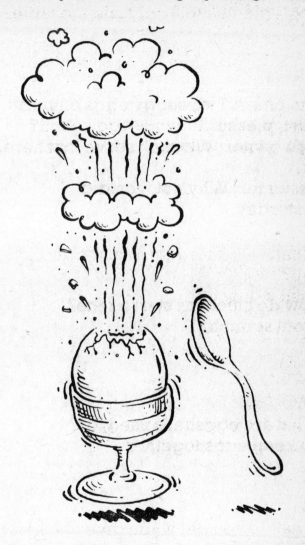

A big eggs–plosion.

Who wrote Great Eggspectations?
Charles Chickens.


Customer: Two soggy eggs on burnt toast, please.
Café owner: We can't serve that here, sir.
Customer: Why not, you did yesterday.


How do chickens start a race?
From scratch.


What are eggshells used for?
To keep eggs together.


Where's the best place to buy eggs?
Henley.

What tells jokes and lays eggs?
*A comedi-hen.*

What do you get if you cross a piece of toast
with an egg and an eiderdown?
*Breakfast in bed.*

What do you get
if you cross a hen
with a banjo?
*A chicken that
plucks itself.*

What do you get if you cross a hen with
some gunpowder?
*An eggs-plosion.*

Why did the chicken run onto the football
pitch?
*Because the referee blew for a foul.*

How does a wally make scrambled eggs?
*He holds the pan and gets two friends to shake
him violently.*

'Doctor, doctor, my tongue is as yellow as custard and my legs are as wobbly as jelly.'
*'Don't worry – you're just a trifle ill.'*

'Doctor, doctor, this banana diet isn't working on me.'
*'Stop scratching and come down from the curtains.'*

'Doctor, doctor, I've got bananas growing out of my ears.'
*'Good gracious, how did that happen?'*
'I don't know, I planted apples,'

APPLE SEEDS

What's yellow and sneaks around the kitchen?
*Custard spies.*

What's yellow and round and 5 miles in circumference?
*The Great Ball of China.*

What's yellow,
comes from Peru,
and is totally unknown?
*Euston Bear.*

What's yellow and never talks to anyone?
*A lemon sole.*

What's yellow and stays hot in the fridge?
*Mustard.*

What's yellow, full of holes, and holds water?
*A wet sponge.*

What's yellow, weighs 4 tons, and has a blocked trunk?
*An elephant drowning in a bowl of custard.*

'Doctor, doctor, I feel like a yellow
snooker ball.'
*'Well get to the back of the queue (cue).'*

'Doctor, doctor, for the last ten years my
brother has believed he is a hen.'
*'Goodness gracious, why didn't you
come to me sooner?'*
'We needed the eggs.'

What do you get if you cross a daffodil with a calculator?
*A flower with square roots.*

'Doctor, doctor, my mother thinks I'm crazy because I prefer yellow socks to grey ones.'
*'What's crazy about that? So do I.'*
'Really? How do you like them – fried or boiled?'

'Doctor, doctor, I feel like a banana.'
*'So do I – get me one too.'*

'Doctor, doctor, I feel like custard'
*'Sit down, man, and don't be so thick.'*

Why don't grapefruit tie their own
shoelaces?
*If you had a shape like a grapefruit, you
couldn't see your feet either.*

How can you tell that strawberries are
lazy?
*They spend their entire lives in bed.*

What is an overweight pumpkin
called?

*A plumpkin.*

Why do boy pumpkins wear blue
bow- ties?
*So you can tell them from girl
pumpkins.*

What's yellow and sweet and holds
baby monkeys?
*An ape-ricot.*


What's yellow, furry and rides along
the sea-shore?
*A peach buggy.*

What's red and green and wears
boxing gloves?
*Fruit punch.*

What's brown,
mad and lives in
South America?
*A Brazil nut.*

What's green
and hairy and
takes aspirin?
*A gooseberry
with a headache.*

**What's purple and close to France?**
*Grape Britain.*

**What's purple and glows in the dark?**
*A 100 watt grape.*

**What's round
and purple
and barks at people?**
*A Grape Dane.*

**Who swings through the vines?**
*Tarzan of the Grapes.*

What's purple and 8,000 kilometres long?
*The Grape Wall of China.*

What's fruity and burns cakes?
*Alfred the Grape.*

What's purple and burns?
*The Grape Fire of London.*

What's purple and ruled Russian?
*Catherine the Grape.*

'Mummy, mummy, there's a man at the door selling honey.'
*'Tell him to buzz off.'*

What did the mother bee say to the baby bee?
*'Don't be naughty, honey, just beehive yourself while I comb your hair.'*

Why do bees have sticky hair?
*Because they have honey combs.*

What are the bees on strike for?
*More honey and shorter flowers.*

What do bees do with honey?
*They cell it.*

What did the bee say to the flower?
*'Hello, honey.'*

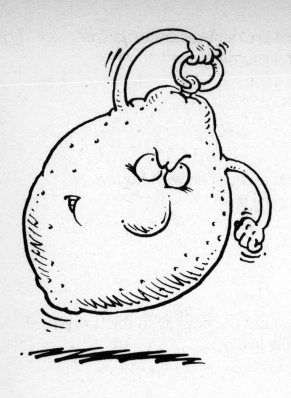

What's yellow and highly dangerous?
*A hand grenade disguised as a lemon.*

'Holmes, why is that door painted yellow?'
*'It's a lemon-entry, my dear Watson.'*

What is the difference between a lemon and a melon?
*The order in which the letters are written.*

How do you make a lemon drop?
*Shake the tree.*

When a lemon calls for help, what should you give it?
*Lemonade*

What do you get if you cross a lemon
with a dinosaur?
*A dinosour*.

What's yellow, sour, and wobbles
all over the road?

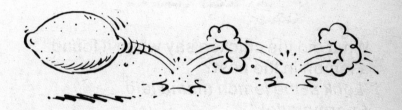

*A lemon with a puncture.*

What did the chicken say when it found
a lemon in the nest?
*'Look at the lemon mama laid
(marmalade).'*

What's furry, whiskered, and sucks
lemons?
*A sour puss.*

What did the
elephant say
to the lemon?
*Let's play squash.*

Did you ever see a lemon peel?
*No, but I once saw an apple turnover.*

What's yellow and flickers?
*A lemon with a loose connection.*

Knock, knock.
– *Who's there?*
Bab.
– *Bab who?*
Bab Boone is
a real ape.

What do you
call a monkey
with a sweet tooth?
*A meringue- outang.*

What is the difference between a monkey, a bald man and the Prince of Wales?
*A monkey is a hairy parent; a bald man has no hair apparent, and The Prince of Wales is the heir apparent.*

Knock, knock.
– *Who's there?*
Beryl.
– *Beryl who?*
Beryl load of monkeys.

What did the monkey say as he fell out of the tree?
*Aaarrrggghh!*

What does the government use when it takes a census of all the monkeys in the zoo?
*An ape recorder!*

What do you get
if you cross
a spanner with
a chimpanzee?
*A monkey wrench.*

What's green and swings through the trees?
*A septic monkey.*

What keys are furry?
*Monkeys.*

What do you get if you cross a monkey with a Scottish dance and a joker?
*An ape- reel fool.*

What do you get
if you cross a
monkey with an idiot?
*A chumpanzee.*

How do you catch a monkey?
*Hang upside down from a tree and
make a noise like a banana.*

What's the definition of guerilla
warfare?
*Monkeys throwing coconuts at each
other!*

'Is that your own face, or are you
breaking it in for a baboon?'

How do monkeys keep rumours
circulating?
*On the apevine.*

What's purple
and has
eight legs?
*An octoplum.*

Who was purple and discovered America in
1492?
*Christopher Plumbus.*

Who is purple, has scars on his head, and
frightens people?
*Frankenplum.*

Why is a plum a good museum keeper?
*Plum preserves.*

What do you
get if you cross
a plum and
a tiger?
*A purple
people eater.*

Which was the smallest plum?
*Tom Plum.*

What plum wrote under an alias?
*Nom de plum.*


What is Dracula's favourite pudding?
*I scream.*


What do climbers eat for dessert?
*Rock cakes.*


What do you do if
someone offers
you rock cakes
for pudding?
*Take your pick.*

What's soft and yellow and comes from outer space?
*A martian mellow.*


What's the favorite dessert in Wales?
*Taffy apples.*


What is a lawyer's favorite pudding?
*Suet.*


What pudding do you get if you cross a football team with an ice cream?
*Aston Vanilla.*

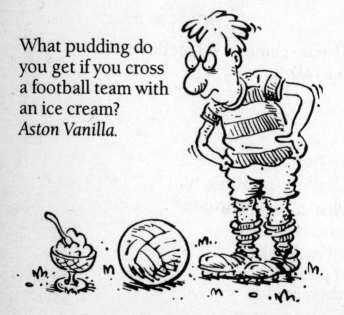

What do the Scots have for pudding?
*Tartan custard.*

What's yellow and highly dangerous?
*Shark-infested custard.*

Knock, knock.
– *Who's there?*
Jaws.
– *Jaws who?*
Jaws truly.

What do you get if you cross an
American president with a shark?
*Jaws Washington.*

What do you get if you cross a pop
singer with a shark?
*Boy Jaws.*

What do you get if you cross a shark
with a padlock?
*Lock-jaws.*

What do you get if you cross a shark
with the Loch Ness Monster?
*Loch Jaws!*

What do you get
if you cross a
shark with a snowman?
*Frost-bite.*

What happened to the yacht that sank in shark-infested waters?
*It came back with a skeleton crew.*

What eats its victims two by two?
*Noah's shark.*

What shark never swims?
*A dead one.*

'Waiter, waiter, there's a fly in my custard!'
*'That's all right, sir, the spider will get it.'*

'Waiter, waiter, there's a fly in my custard!'
'I know, it's the rotten fruit that attracts them.'

'Waiter, waiter, there's a fly in my custard!'
'If you throw it a pea it will play water polo.'

What's yellow and highly dangerous?
A man-eating duster.

If a buttercup is yellow, what colour is a hiccup?
*Burple.*

Did you hear about the Rubik Cube for wallies? *It's yellow on all six sides.*

What do you get when you jump in the Yellow River?
*Wet.*

Police: What gear were you in at the time of the accident?
Motorist: *A yellow pullover, if it makes any difference.*

What's tall, yellow and smells nice?
*A giraff-odil.*

What's yellow and sweet and swings from tree to tree?
*Tarzipan.*

'I suppose your new baby brother is a lovely pink child?'
*'No, he's an 'orrible yeller!'*

What happened to the frog when he parked on the yellow line?
*He got toad away.*

'Why is your dog wearing yellow shoes?'
*'Because his black ones are at the mender's.'*

What's yellow and brown and dances around toadstools?
*A brownie with jaundice.*

What's yellow, green, blue, purple, brown, black and white, and good on the draw?
*A box of crayons.*

What colour is a shout?
*Yell-oh.*

What's small, yellow, and eats cakes?
*A yellow dwarf cake-eater.*

What's big and yellow and eats rocks?
*A giant yellow rock eater.*

What leaves yellow footprints all over the sea-bed?
*A lemon sole.*

Why do traffic wardens have yellow lines on their hats?
*To stop people from parking on their heads.*

A women with a baby in her arms was sitting in a station waiting room, sobbing miserably. A porter came up to her and asked what the trouble was. 'Some people were in here just now and they were so rude about my little boy,' she cried. 'They all said he was ugly.' *There, there, don't cry,* said the porter kindly. *Shall I get you a nice cup of tea?* 'Thank you, that would be nice,' replied the woman, wiping her eyes. 'You're very kind.' *That's all right. Don't mention it,* said the porter. *While I'm at it, by the way, would you like a banana for your gorilla?*

Why did King Kong climb Cleopatra's Needle?
*To get his kite.*

Where does a gorilla sleep?
*Anywhere it wants to.*

Why did the gorilla lie in the middle of the path?

*To trip up the ants.*

What would you get if you cross a gorilla with a bell?
*A ding-dong King Kong.*

What do gorillas sing at Christmas time?
*'Jungle bells, Jungle bells . . .'*

Why don't
gorillas eat
penguins?
*Because they
can't get the
wrappers
off.*

Why do gorillas scratch themselves?
*Because they're the only ones who
know where they itch.*

What's the difference between a biscuit
and a gorilla?
*Ever tried dunking a gorilla?*

BOY 1: I'm going to keep this gorilla
under my bed.
BOY 2: *But what about the smell?*
BOY 1: He'll just have to get used to it.

What do you call a gorilla who works as
a car mechanic?
*A grease monkey.*

What do you call
a gorilla with two
bananas in his ears?
*Anything you like,
because he can't
hear you.*

What do you do if you find a gorilla in
your bed?
*Sleep somewhere else.*

What is big
and hairy
and flies
at Mach 2?
*King Kongcorde.*

What is big and hairy and goes round and round?
*A gorilla in a revolving door.*

Who rings the bell twice then knocks down the door?
*The Avon gorilla.*

JANE: I can trace my ancestry all the way back to royalty.
JILL: *King Kong?*

Why did King Kong join the army?
*He wanted to study gorilla warfare.*

What's big and hairy and climbs up the Empire State Building?
*Queen Kong.*